APPLE WATCH

SERIES 9

USER GUIDE

The Comprehensive Practical Manual To Mastering The Apple Watch Series 9 For Beginners & Seniors With Step By Step WatchOS 10 Instructions, Tips & Tricks

By

Williams M. Brown

Table Of Contents

INTRODUCTION

On September 12, 2023, with the new and exciting iPhone 15 series, Apple officially unveiled the Apple Watch Series 9, their current premium wristwatch.

The Apple Watch 9 this year is just an incremental upgrade that sees a speed boost from the new S9 processor—which is based on the A15—thanks to a redesign. Plus, with the most recent WatchOS update, you can enjoy speedier on-device Siri, a brighter screen, and a new motion called Double Tap.

Released Date

Announcing the Apple Watch Series 9 on September 12, 2023. September 22, 2023, was the commencement of general availability in retailers.

Device family	Announcement	Market release
Apple Watch Series 4	September 12, 2018	September 21, 2018
Apple Watch Series 5	September 10, 2019	September 20, 2019
Apple Watch Series 6	September 15, 2020	September 18, 2020
Apple Watch Series 7	September 14, 2021	October 15, 2021
Apple Watch Series 8	September 7, 2022	September 16, 2022
Apple Watch Series 9	September 12, 2023 (date of next Apple event)	September 22, 2023

Price

Regarding pricing, there have been no changes; the Apple Watch Series 9 is identical to its predecessor.

Series 9 Apple Watches, like earlier premium models, start at $399. An Apple Watch with cellular capabilities will naturally cost more. The size of the watch is another factor that determines its pricing.

Apple Watch model	41mm GPS only	45mm GPS only	41mm GPS + Cellular	45mm GPS + Cellular
Apple Watch Series 7	$399	$429	$499	$529
Apple Watch Series 8	$399	$429	$499	$529
Apple Watch Series 9	$399	$429	$499	$529

Design

Even in terms of design, we don't have any major surprises. The Series 9 Apple Watch is visually similar to its predecessors, with two distinct case sizes (41 mm and 45 mm) and an instantly identifiable rectangular shape.

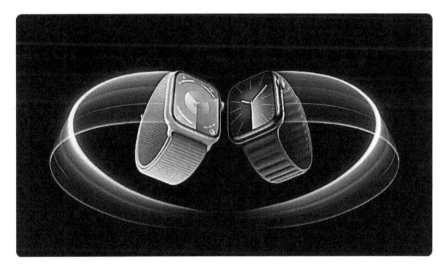

The case material is customizable, giving you the usual options of aluminum or stainless steel.

The Apple Watch Series 9 is available in a rainbow of colors, including pink, to match the iPhone 15's color scheme. Aside from that, you may choose Product (RED), Midnight, Silver, or Starlight.

The digital crown and buttons have also remained unchanged.

Series 9 Watches Include All New Bands.

Apple has recently made efforts to reduce its environmental impact, and the tech giant is now ramping up its efforts even more. Apple has eliminated the use of leather bands from the Series 9 in favor of new, eco-friendly bands. As an example, Apple's first carbon-neutral device is the Series 9, which includes a new Sport Loop.

There are also new eco-friendly goods from the Nike and Hermès partnerships.

These are the Nike bands that are now environmentally friendly

Apple claims that the new FineWoven material, which is made of 68% post-consumer recycled materials, will take the place of leather bands. Although we are now sold out of leather bands, we do have Magnetic Link and Modern Buckle bands in store.

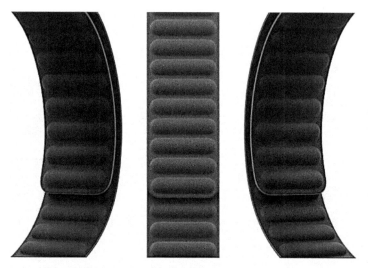

Apple's new FineWoven bands. The picture shows the FineWoven band with the Magnetic Link

Technical Specifications For The Screen

Apple and wearable display technology took a giant leap forward with the release of the Series 7 Apple Watch in 2021. In contrast to the Series 6, this model's screen is larger and the bezels are much slimmer. In contrast, the Series 8 maintained essentially the same display as its predecessors; the only real difference between the two was the design of the watch faces. The Always-On Retina display of the Series 8 is resistant to dust and cracks, and it becomes pleasantly bright when exposed to natural light.

Apple has shown its appreciation for the Apple Watch Series 9 display by upgrading it. Its maximum brightness has been doubled from the Series 8 to 2,000 nits. The screen otherwise remains unchanged from its predecessor.

Power Source

Apple should seriously consider improving the battery life of its Apple Watches. Although the new Ultra 2 and the Apple Watch Ultra both have longer battery lives, not everyone is interested in wearing such a large wristwatch all day and night. The amount of time an Apple Watch can last on a single charge has hardly changed so far. Even with the Series 9, this trend continues.

With its new Low Power Mode, the Series 9 may extend its battery life to 36 hours, in addition to the 18 hours that the regular watch can endure.

When it comes to charging, the Series 8 can go from zero to eighty percent in around forty-five minutes (with an Apple USB-C Magnetic Fast Charging Cable and a fast charging brick), according to official Apple literature. That being said, we also think the Series 9 is really good.

Features And Software

Allow me to briefly go over the new chip that powers the Series 9 before we get into the features. The S9, as we said at the outset of this piece, is based on the A15. Compared to the S8 processor, this one contains 60% more transistors, making it quicker and more powerful. The new four-core Neural Engine further accelerates machine learning activities by a factor of two to three.

Shown during the occasion, the new Double Tap gesture is the product of the new Neural Engine. Two taps with the index finger and thumb are now sufficient to operate the watch's main functionalities.

You may now answer and end calls and use the new gesture to control the primary button in apps, allowing you to perform things like play/pause music, stop a timer, or snooze an alarm.

Introducing the second-generation Ultra Wideband, your Apple Watch Series 9 can now pinpoint the exact location of your iPhone with more accuracy. The integration of HomePod enables you to manage the music playing from the Now Playing screen of the Series 9, and features like precise finding utilize your Apple Watch to lead you to your iPhone. These are all made possible by this.

Accessing and logging health data is now possible with on-device Siri as well. Improvements in speed and security have been made to on-device processing. If you want to know how many hours you slept last night or how far along you are in the process of closing your Activity ring, you may ask Siri to inform you. Apple has promised that "later this year" users would be able to ask Siri questions about their health records.

The Series 9 carries on the legacy of Apple Watches' famous health-related functions. The Series 9 retains all of the standard features seen on Apple's higher-end watches. Among these are the following: Crash Detection, Heart Rate, Sleep, and Emergency SOS.

Series 9 models now have the same temperature monitoring capabilities as Series 8 models, which is great news for women's health.

Naturally, the Series 9 will also come with a plethora of exercises, as all of Apple's premium watches do.

With WatchOS 10, The Apple Watch Series 9 Will Run Smoothly.

Apple introduced watchOS 10 earlier this year; the Series 9 comes with the OS preinstalled. The upgraded operating system adds many practical functions to the watch. At the outset, there's a revamped display that lets you access widgets right from the watch face. Along with watchOS 10, you also get Smart Stack.

However, there's more! As part of watchOS 10, Apple revamped several core applications. Upon the release of watchOS 10, some stock applications will get cosmetic changes. These include Weather, Stocks, Home, Maps, Messages, and the World Clock.

Significant enhancements are also being made to the activities. New metrics and statistics display for cyclists will be available on Apple Watch devices with watchOS 10. For instance, when you start a cycling activity on your Apple Watch, it will be synced with your iPhone as a Live Activity. This activity will take you to a large screen where you can see important metrics like your heart rate, distance traveled, average speed, and current speed.

Finally, Palette and Snoopy & Woodstock are two new watch faces that will be available in the update.

SOME FEATURES OF APPLE WATCH SERIES 9

The All New S9 Chip

The Apple Watch Series 9 is the product of silicon created by Apple, which makes it more powerful, easier to operate, and faster. The new dual-core CPU outperforms the S8 chip by 60% thanks to its 5.6 billion transistors. A state-of-the-art four-core Neural Engine processes machine learning tasks twice as quickly as before. Among the many new capabilities it enables is the double-tap gesture.

Gestures (The Two-Finger)

Even with a full hand, you can utilize the new Replay, Play, and Pause gestures on the Apple Watch. With only two taps of your index and thumb, you can do a whole lot more, including answer calls, open alerts, play and pause music, and much more besides.

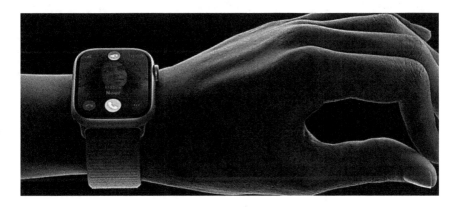

- Effortlessly move about the house while listening to music.
- While paddling, take a phone call.
- Put a timer on high while you bake a pie.
- Respond to a message while taking the dog for a walk.
- As you hold your toddler, check the contents of your Smart Stack.

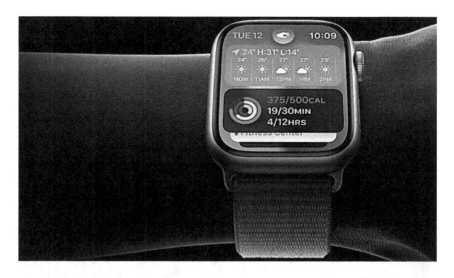

A Dual-LED Screen

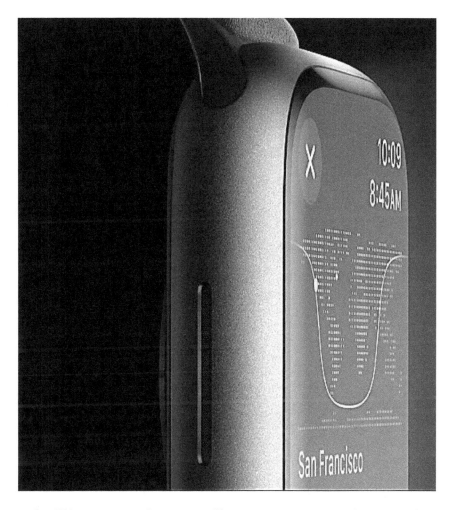

A brilliant new feature allows you to see the watch's brightness from the side view.

With an increase to 2000 nits, the unique display technology of the Series 9 makes it easier to view in direct sunshine, double the maximum brightness of the Series 8. Also, it works well in dark environments, like a movie theater, thanks to its 1 nit dimming capability.

Your iPhone Lost And Precisely Found

Precision Finding, another feature made possible by the second-generation Ultra Wideband processor, can now pinpoint your iPhone's location and provide directions to it.1 You can go very near to it and then focus on it with the assistance of haptic feedback, an auditory chirp, and a visual signal.

WatchOS 10

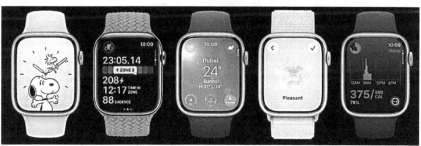

The most recent update to watchOS, 10, expands the capabilities of your screen beyond anything before. There is now more information available at a look thanks to many app redesigns. From any face of the watch, you may access the Smart Stack with widgets that show you current information by spinning the

Digital Crown. With only the flick of a wrist, you can now track not only your physical health, but also your mental and visual well-being.

Apple's First Carbon-Neutral Product.

Constant innovation in materials, renewable energy, and eco-friendly shipping has made carbon-neutral band and case options for the Apple Watch a reality.

Your emotional and physical well-being may be better understood with the aid of the Apple Watch. We ensure the privacy and security of any health data. The decision to disclose to a healthcare practitioner, friends, or family members is ultimately yours to make.

Health

Instantaneous insights.

Your emotional and physical well-being may be better understood with the aid of the Apple Watch. We ensure the privacy and security of any health data. You get to decide when it's time to share with your healthcare practitioner, loved ones, or friends.

Keeps An Eye On Your Emotions. The ECG app allows the Apple Watch Series 9 to produce an electrocardiogram (ECG) that is comparable to a single-lead ECG. Additionally, if your heart rate is abnormally high or low, or if it beats in an irregular rhythm, the Heart Rate app may notify you.

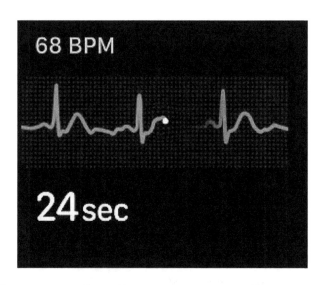

Check Your Blood Oxygen Levels. I am really astounded by this innovation. The incredible sensor and software in the Apple Watch Series 9 allow you to collect background and on-demand readings of your blood oxygen levels at any time of day or night.

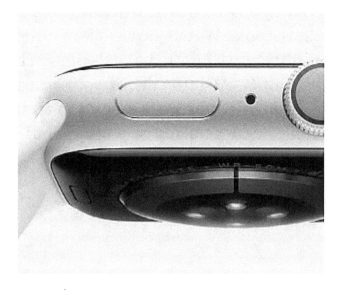

The Machine Of Dreams. In addition to tracking the amount of time you sleep, the Sleep app has other features. You may learn more about your sleep cycle, including the duration of each stage (REM, Core, and Deep) and any possible wake-up times, by reviewing your sleep log.

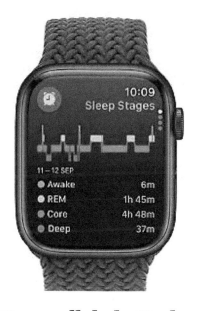

Gain An Unparalleled Understanding Of Your Cycle. A revolutionary sensor in the Apple Watch Series 9 monitors your core body temperature while you sleep, allowing you to see variations over time. To aid with family planning, 7 Cycle Tracking analyzes this information to provide a historical estimate of when you probably ovulated.8

TODAY, 12 SEP

Record How You're Feeling. To keep track of your daily mood and fleeting emotions, just open the Mindfulness app on your Apple Watch and swipe through the visually appealing options to choose how you're feeling. Keep the complexities and alerts on your watch face constant.

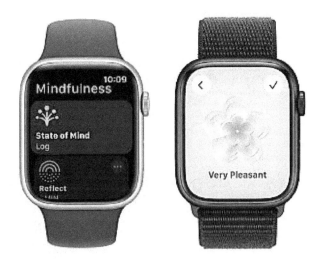

Link Everything At The Pace Of Life.

With the Apple Watch, you can stay in touch with the people and things that matter to you from the palm of your hand. Even when your iPhone isn't in the room, you can still accomplish all of that with a cellular subscription.

The Independence Of Cells. Respond to a signal from the wayside. Respond to a text message when you're out and about. Pay attention to a signal in the yard. Can you still contact me? Sure thing.

Play Audio Files And Listen To Podcasts Online. Stream millions of songs of inspiring music on Apple Music.10 Alternatively, you may listen to recently-edited episodes.

Quick Cash. Keep your cash and cards close at hand. Use Apple Pay on the go with your wrist.11

Follow The Motion Of Your Wrist. Haptic feedback is now an option in Apple Maps' turn-by-turn guidance. To the point where you won't need to check your watch to see the precise destination.

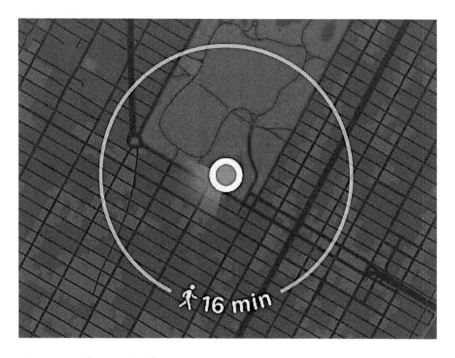

Strength training

With a simple touch, it will be ready for any exercise routine you can imagine. Access all the metrics that matter for staying motivated in perspectives that you can customize. And long-lasting reliability so you can push yourself to your limits without worrying about your Apple Watch breaking.

Hop, Skip, And Run. With the Apple Watch, you may exercise in different types of methods, including strength training, high-intensity interval training (HIIT), Pilates, and meditation, and it will track all the important metrics for you.

Extremely Difficult. Apple Watch is quite durable and won't break easily because of its flat base, sturdy design, and front crystal. Furthermore, it can endure water pressures of up to 50 meters.

Views Of Workouts. Observe everything. Try everything. While you're exercising, you may observe all the necessary stats on the screen at once, including Heart Rate Zones and personalized intervals. To access stats like splits and segments, elevation, and activity rings, just spin the digital crown.

Actual, Ongoing Action. A Live Activity notification will be sent to your iPhone whenever you start a ride on your wristwatch. By tapping it, you may make it fill the whole screen, making it simpler to see your numbers while riding.

Safety

Series 9 can summon assistance whenever you need it, whether it is in the event of a fall, automobile accident, or other emergency.

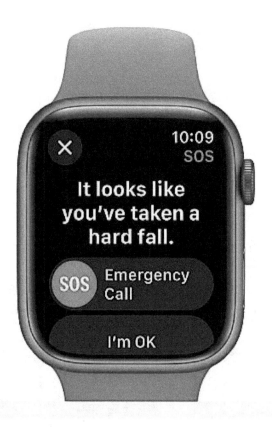

Identifying Crashes. Your Apple Watch Series 9 has the ability to detect whether you're involved in a severe car accident. When a catastrophic accident is detected, it will automatically notify your emergency contacts, relay your location to dispatchers, and connect you with emergency personnel.

We detect falls. After a serious fall, your Apple Watch Series 9 can alert authorities if you lose the ability to speak.

Timely alert. With Emergency SOS, your Apple Watch will notify local emergency services and reveal your position when you make a call. Holding down the side button will bring up a help menu.

CHAPTER ONE

HOW TO PAIR AND SET UP THE APPLE WATCH SERIES 9

- To begin, locate the button under the digital crown—the side button—and push and hold it to power the watch.
- To verify whether your iPhone's Bluetooth and Wi-Fi are turned on, go to the Control Center.
- Hold the watch close to your iPhone until you've confirmed this. An alert should now appear on your iPhone to confirm the detection of a nearby Apple Watch. Click the Proceed button.
- No need to fret if you don't encounter any pop-ups; just launch the Watch app on your phone and choose the "Set Up for Me" option.
- After then, your Apple Watch Series 9 screen will show an animation. This requires you to use your iPhone for scanning. There you have it.

- After the scan is finished, your iPhone will take you to the setup page, and may download updates. Hit the "Set Up Apple Watch" button over here.

- After that, you'll see a series of displays that will direct you to do something. Upon accepting the Terms of Service, you will be able to access the following screens: hand selection, data sharing options, GPS permissions, and font size.

- Stepping beyond this will bring you to other crucial features, such as the ability to create a password and input personal information for activity monitoring.

- Here you may record information about your daily routine, such as the number of calories you want to burn, the number of steps you want to take, your weight, and the amount of time you want to spend exercising. This is a great gamified approach to reaching your health goals—closing the three rings.

- Here you will also learn the meaning of the three rings; the red one represents your daily calorie burn, the green one your training minutes, and the blue one closes when you reach your Stand Goal.

- An excellent addition that will serve as a reminder to get up and move around is the Stand Goal. The optimal setting is once every hour, but you may choose whatever number you choose. Because it allows you to simply get up and stretch your legs, this function is particularly beneficial for the health of those who have sedentary occupations.

- After that, a screen will appear asking whether you would want to activate the blood oxygen sensor immediately or wait to set it up. If you want to know your blood oxygen levels, you should utilize this function manually. When set to all-day monitoring, it tends to impair battery life.
- The next step, which we highly encourage, is to enable automatic updates for your Watch Series 9. Next, you'll see a screen where you may configure your heart rate notifications. You'll also have the option to change this in the settings later on.
- The next screen will show the Emergency SOS and Fall Detection options; after reading them, click Continue.

- Press the Continue button when prompted by the always-on display; this is a convenient method to see alerts and other information like the date and time without waking up the screen.

- When you install third-party applications on your iPhone, do you want them to instantly be added to your Apple Watch? To enable or disable that feature, go to the next screen. We advise that you continue to manually install applications on your Watch Series 9 (via the Watch app on iOS) since there are many types of apps that you may not want the Watch app for.

- The next page gives you the option to see your applications in either a grid or list format.
- Your Apple Watch Series 9 will finally start synchronizing. You may as well press the Get to Know Your Watch button as syncing takes a while.
- At the Welcome screen, which appears once synchronization is finished, press OK.

- At last, you'll reach the Watch app's main interface. Scroll down to the bottom of the page and you'll notice three tabs: My Watch, Face Gallery, and Discover.
- Accessibility settings, app management, and notification preferences are just a few of the

many options available to you in the My Watch area of your Apple Watch Series 9.

- You may choose and personalize the look of your downloaded watch faces in the Face Gallery.
- In the Discover section of your Apple Watch, you'll find a wealth of information, including several mini-articles that detail how to do various functions on the Watch Series 9.

Updates to your most used applications, like as Workouts, Messages, Activity, Maps, Weather, and more, as well as new watch faces, redesigns of current apps, and more tailored information, are all part of WatchOS 10. Take your time getting to know your new wristwatch if this is your first Apple Watch; the subtle touches that Apple has included will thrill you. The watch has a long lifespan with proper care and protection, but if anything does happen to it—you'll be glad you upgraded to the latest Apple Watch!

HOW TO CHARGE APPLE WATCH SERIES 9

Install The Power Adapter

1. Keep your device and its charging cord on a level surface in an area with good ventilation. Both the Apple Watch Magnetic Charging Cable and the Apple Watch Magnetic Fast Charger to USB-C Cable come standard with your Apple Watch. The former is compatible with all models, while the latter is exclusive to the Apple Watch Series 7, 8, and 9. It also works with the MagSafe Duo Charger, which is sold separately, and the Apple Watch.Attach the charging cord to the power adapter, which is available for purchase separately.

2. Find an electrical outlet and insert the adaptor.

An 18W USB-C power adapter is necessary for fast charging. Quick charging for Apple Watch is covered in detail in an article on Apple Support.

Note: Not all areas provide fast charging.

Get The Apple Watch Ready To Charge.

Use either the magnetic charging cable (for earlier models) or the supplied cable (for Apple Watch Series 7 and later) to connect your wristwatch to a USB-C port. Make sure your charging cable is in the right place by magnetically attaching the concave end to the back of your Apple Watch.

Unless you've enabled silent mode, your Apple Watch will make a beep sound and display a charging symbol on the front as it begins to charge. The Apple Watch's charging symbol will be green while the battery life is high and red when it's low. When the Apple Watch is in Low Power Mode, a charging symbol will appear on the screen.

It is possible to charge your Apple Watch by laying it flat, band removed or on its side.

+ Position your Apple Watch so that it lies flat on the MagSafe Duo Charger or Apple Watch Magnetic Charging Dock.

- When your battery life is short, you can see a picture of the Apple Watch Magnetic Charging Cable or the Apple Watch Magnetic Fast Charger to USB-C Cable on the screen. Refer to the page on Apple Support for more details. When the Apple Watch refuses to power on or charge.

Apple Watch Series 9

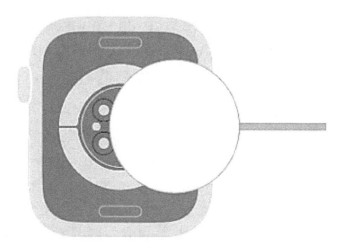

Apple Watch Series 8

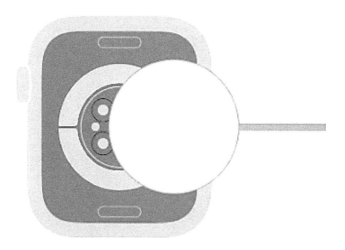

Apple Watch SE (2ⁿᵈ Generation)

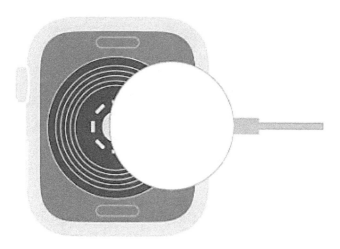

Apple Watch Series 7

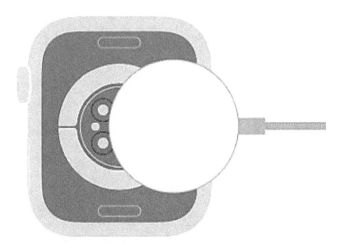

Apple Watch Series 6

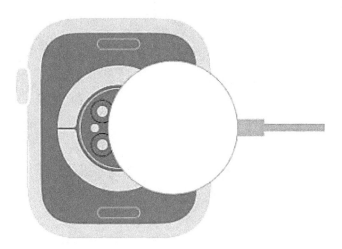

Apple Watch SE

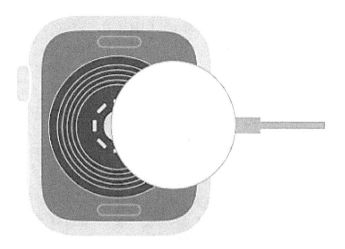

Apple Watch Series 4 And Apple Watch Series 5

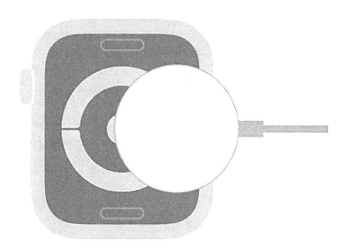

Evaluate The Battery Life

To access the Control Center and see the remaining battery life, push the side button. You may make checking the battery life easier by including a battery indicator on the watch face.

View the percentage of remaining battery life.

Reduce Energy Use

Enabling Low Power Mode will help you save battery life. This disables the Always On Display feature, as well as the background measurements of heart rate and blood oxygen levels, and alerts related to heart rate. Notifications from other sources may take longer to arrive, emergency warnings could not get out at all, and certain Wi-Fi and cellular networks have restrictions. Unless you need cellular data, such as when sending a message or streaming music, it is off.

Note: After the battery reaches 80% charge, Low Power Mode will be disabled.

- To access the Control Center, press the side button.
- To activate Low Power Mode, tap the battery percentage.
- Once you've made your selection, scroll down and touch Turn On to confirm.

   You have the option to turn it on for one, two, or three days by tapping the Turn On For button.

Advice: Within the Control Center, you'll see a percentage that you can tap to see the remaining battery life of your AirPods or any other battery-operated device that has been connected with your Apple Watch using Bluetooth. Next, turn the Digital Crown to check the remaining battery life of your headphones.

Your Apple Watch will notify you and ask you to enter Low Power Mode when the battery life drops to 10% or below.

Go Back To The Standard Power Setting

- To access the Control Center, press the side button.
- To disable Low Power Mode, tap the battery percentage.

Keep Track Of How Much Time Has Passed Since The Previous Battery Charge.

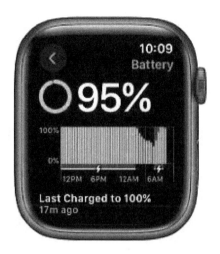

- ◆ Go to your Apple Watch's Settings.
- ◆ Press the power button.

In addition to showing the amount of battery life that is still usable, the Battery screen also includes a graph that displays the charging history of the battery and describes the last time it was charged.

Assess The Condition Of The Battery.

Your Apple Watch's battery life may be seen in comparison to its initial state.

- ◆ Go to your Apple Watch's Settings.
- ◆ Select Battery, followed by Battery Health.

Apple Watch notifies you when your battery life is becoming low, giving you the chance to look into your servicing choices.

Efficiently Charge Batteries

By analyzing your charging habits, the Apple Watch may delay charging beyond 80 percent until you're ready to use it, therefore reducing battery aging. This feature is made possible by on-device machine learning.

- Go to your Apple Watch's Settings.
- Select Battery, followed by Battery Health.
- Enable Optimal Charging for Batteries.

Stop Applications From Automatically Renewing Themselves.

Although the previously used app does not stay open or use any system resources when you move to another app, it may continue to "refresh" in the background to look for updates and new material.

Background applications that refresh might use electricity. You may disable this feature to extend the life of your battery.

- Go to your Apple Watch's Settings.
- To refresh the app's background, go to General > Background Refresh.
- To stop all applications from refreshing, disable Background App Refresh. Alternately,

you may disable refresh for certain applications by scrolling down.

Note: Even when you turn off the background app refresh feature, apps that have complications on the current watch face will keep refreshing.

CHAPTER TWO

HOW TO LOCK OR UNLOCK APPLE WATCH SERIES 9

Get Apple Watch Unlocked

Entering the passcode manually or having it open automatically when you unlock your iPhone are two ways to access your Apple Watch.

- ***Please Input The Password:*** Once the Apple Watch has woken up, input the passcode.
- ***Get Your Apple Watch Unlocked At The Same Time As Your iPhone:*** Navigate to My Watch in the Apple Watch app on your iPhone. From there, hit Passcode. Finally, enable Unlock with iPhone.

  To unlock your Apple Watch, you'll need to bring your iPhone within the standard Bluetooth range of your wristwatch, which is about 33 feet (10 meters). To unlock your Apple Watch while Bluetooth is turned off, just input the passcode on the device.

Advice: It's recommended that you use a separate password for your Apple Watch and iPhone.

However, your Apple Watch passcode might vary from your iPhone passcode.

Update The Password

If you'd want to modify the passcode that was set up when you first got your Apple Watch, here's how:

- Go to your Apple Watch's Settings.
- To change your passcode, press the Passcode button, and then follow the on-screen instructions.

You may also use your iPhone's Apple Watch app to achieve the same function. To change your watch's passcode, go to My Watch, then tap the Passcode. Everything is laid out for you on the screen.

Hint: To enable a passcode that is more than four digits long, go to your Apple Watch's Settings app, choose Passcode, and finally, disable Simple Passcode.

Activate The Passcode

- Go to your Apple Watch's Settings.
- Select Passcode, and then select Turn Passcode Off.

Other options include opening the Apple Watch app on your iPhone, tapping My Watch, then tapping Passcode, and finally tapping Turn Passcode Off.

Important: Some functions may not be accessible if you choose to deactivate your passcode. Some examples of this include the inability to utilize Apple Pay or to unlock a Mac using an Apple Watch.

If A Basic Passcode Doesn't Work Or If You've Forgotten Your Passcode,

If an institution, such as a school or workplace, is in charge of your synced iPhone, you may not be able to use the Simple Passcode or Turn Passcode Off options. Make sure you consult with the upper management of your company.

Secure Automatically

When you're not actively using it, your Apple Watch will lock itself by default. The following steps will allow you to modify the wrist detection setting.

- Go to your Apple Watch's Settings.
- Select Passcode, and then toggle Wrist Detection to On or Off.

These Apple Watch functions are affected when wrist detection is turned off:

- When you double-click the side button on your Apple Watch to approve a purchase using Apple Pay, you'll be asked to enter your password.
- Certain activity metrics cannot be obtained.
- Notifications and heart rate monitoring are disabled.
- The automatic locking and unlocking of the Apple Watch has been disabled.
- Even after detecting a heavy impact fall, the Apple Watch would not immediately dial 911.

Lock Manually

You need to disable wrist detection if you want to lock your Apple Watch manually. (Go to your Apple Watch's Settings, search for Passcode, then disable Wrist Detection.)

- To access the Control Center, press the side button.
- Select the option to Lock.

When you next want to access your Apple Watch, you'll be prompted to enter your passcode.

If You Forget Your Passcode

Erasing your Apple Watch is the only option if you can't remember your passcode. Here are several methods to do it:

- Remove the Apple Watch's settings and passcode from your iPhone by disconnecting it from the device. After that, you may pair it again.
- After resetting your Apple Watch, you may link it with your iPhone once again.

Put An End To Apple Watch Unlock Attempts After 10

If your Apple Watch is stolen or lost, you have the option to configure it to delete all data stored on it after ten failed tries to unlock it using the incorrect passcode.

- Go to your Apple Watch's Settings.
- To enable Erase Data, tap Passcode.

HOW TO CUSTOMIZE LANGUAGE AND ORIENTATION ON APPLE WATCH SERIES 9

Select A Language Or Area

If your iPhone supports several languages, you have the option to choose which one will be shown on your Apple Watch.

- On your iPhone, launch the Apple Watch app.
- Select a language by tapping My Watch, then going to General > Language & Region, and tapping Custom.

Press the Add Language button and then choose a language to add.

Note: In languages that are supported by the system and which employ grammatical gender, you have the option to select between three terms of address: feminine, masculine, and neutral.

Orient The Digital Crown Or Swap Wrists

If you want to activate your Apple Watch by raising your wrist, and if you want to change wrists or utilize the Digital Crown on the other side, you may adjust the orientation of your watch so that it responds to your expectations.

- Go to your Apple Watch's Settings.

- Navigate to the General menu and then to the Orientation.

Another option is to access the Apple Watch's settings using the iPhone app. Select My Watch, then go to General > Watch Orientation.

HOW TO CAPTURE SCREENSHOTS ON APPLE WATCH SERIES 9

- Start the iOS Watch app on your iPhone.
- Press the "My Watch" button located in the screen's lower left corner.
- Press on General.
- To enable screenshots, scroll down and touch the switch next to it until it becomes green.

How To Take A Screenshot On Apple Watch

- Determine whatever part of the screen you want to record.
- Hold down the Side button and the Digital Crown with two fingers at the same time.

The successful capture of a screenshot will be shown by a momentary flash of the screen.

Having An Apple Watch Configured For A Loved One

Once you've configured an Apple Watch for a family member, you may enable screenshots:

+ Go into your loved one's Apple Watch's Settings.
+ Select Screenshots from the General menu.
+ Disable screen captures by turning them off.

Your loved one may capture screen captures with their Apple Watch, which will then sync with your iPhone via the Photos app. These are the steps to take a screenshot on an iPhone:

- On your iPhone, launch the Apple Watch app.
- Pick out a family member's Apple Watch by tapping All Watches, then choose Done.
- Navigate to Diagnostic Logs by tapping General.
- Select a screenshot by tapping on it. Press the Share option, and then choose a sharing method to save or share the screenshot.

HOW TO CUSTOMIZE THE BAND OF YOUR APPLE WATCH SERIES 9

Follow these instructions to take your band off.

Be careful to measure the circumference of your Apple Watch before purchasing a replacement band. If the sizes are compatible, you may use a band that was made for an older Apple Watch model with your newer Apple Watch (4th generation and later) or Apple Watch SE.

Cases with a diameter of 38, 40, or 41 millimeters may be used with any band that fits a diameter of 42, 44, or 45 millimeters.

You may use bands designed for 49mm casings with 44mm and 45mm models as well. Bands designed for 44mm or 45mm cases may be used with 49mm cases.

Switch Up Your Tempo

- Using a lint-free microfiber cloth or a soft, cushioned mat, set your Apple Watch face down on a clean surface.
- To disassemble a Link Bracelet, just push the fast-release button located on one of the links.
- Remove the band by sliding it across while holding down the band release button.

If the band still won't slide out, try pressing and holding the band release button again.

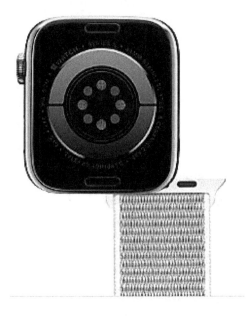

Insert the replacement band until you hear a click, making sure the printed text is facing you the whole time.

If You Have A Braided Solo Loop Or Solo Loop

When putting on or taking off a Braided Solo Loop or Solo Loop, all you have to do is pull it from the bottom to extend it over your wrist.

By Opting For The Milanese Loop

An update to the Milanese Loop in 2018 made it possible to open the band completely by sliding the magnetic closure through the band connector (lug). In earlier Milanese Loop iterations, the closure would not pass through the lug.

By Using The Ocean Band, Alpine Loop, And Trail Loop

For use with the Apple Watch Ultra and subsequent models when partaking in extreme sports and other rough-and-tumble pursuits like jogging, trekking, climbing, kiteboarding, scuba diving, and more, Apple offers three interchangeable bands measuring 49 mm: Ocean, Alpine Loop, and Trail Loop.

You may also use 45mm bands with the Apple Watch Ultra, although those bands are more suited for daily use.

Apple Watch Ultra owners who prefer smaller bands, such as the Braided Solo Loop or Solo Loop, may find that the larger band doesn't quite fit the larger shell. Braided Solo Loop and Solo Loop bands aren't a good fit for Apple Watch Ultra, so try them on first.

Link Bracelet Removal Instructions

Take your Apple Watch band off by first separating the Link Bracelet into its two halves. Be careful not to twist or push the band when you remove it. Follow these procedures carefully so you don't ruin the clasp or band.

Fasten The Butterfly Clasp.

When the butterfly clasp is open, you may close it by folding it in half, one side at a time, till you hear a click.

Keep A Fast Release Button Depressed.

The bracelet's fast-release buttons are located on its interior. Holding one down is all that's required.

Tease The Connections Apart With Care.

As you tug, keep a button for a rapid release depressed. Before you take the band off your Apple Watch, be sure it's split in half.

Take Out Your Band

Remove the band by sliding it across while holding down the band release button.

Find Out More

Never attempt to jam the band into the slot. If you don't hear a click, swing the band left and right to see if it helps. If you position the band appropriately, you may let it slide freely by holding down the band release button.

If the band still won't lock, try pushing it into its center. Gently twisting the band in opposite directions is the next stage. If your Apple Watch band is sliding, remove it from your finger.

CHAPTER THREE

HOW TO USE APPLE WATCH SERIES 9 TO ACCESS APPLICATION

From your Apple Watch's Home Screen, you may access all of your apps. You can quickly access the applications you've recently used using the App Switcher.

Make Use Of A List Or Grid To Showcase Your Applications.

The Home Screen gives you the option to see apps in either a grid or list layout. During the first setup of your Apple Watch, you have the option to personalize the display to your preference. Follow these steps to make a modification at a later time:

- By pressing the Digital Crown located on the face of the watch, you may enter the Home screen.
- After you've scrolled all the way to the bottom of the screen with the Digital Crown, choose between Grid View and List View.

The Settings app also has a View option; from there, you can choose between Grid View or List View by tapping App View.

Launch Programs From The Main Menu

The perspective you pick determines how apps are opened.

- *Visual Representation:* Grid Press on the app's icon. You may see additional applications by turning on the Digital Crown.

View In List Mode: To access an app, spin the Digital Crown and touch it.

Turn the Digital Crown to browse the apps.

Tap to open an app.

When you're done exploring an app, just touch the Digital Crown once to get back to the Home Screen. Repeat the process to switch the face of the watch.

Open An App From The App Switcher

• To access your most recently used applications, open the App Switcher by double-clicking the Digital Crown. Then, rotate the Digital Crown to navigate through your app drawer.

Note: The applications that are now running sessions, such as a navigation session in Maps or a workout session, will be shown at the top of the list.

• Press on an app to launch it.

Turn the Digital Crown to see more apps. Tap one to open it.

Exit An App's Display In The App Switcher

To delete an app, double-click its icon and then swipe left or right to select it. Tap the X after swiping left on the app.

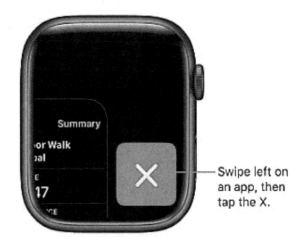

Swipe left on an app, then tap the X.

HOW TO USE CONTROL CENTER ON APPLE WATCH SERIES 9

Your Apple Watch's Control Center makes it simple to do a lot of things, such as check the battery life, quiet the watch, pick a Focus, make it a flashlight, put it in Airplane Mode, activate theater mode, and much more.

Launch Or Reopen The Command Center

- One press of the side button will bring up the Control Center.
- If the Control Center is open, you may close it by removing your wrist from the screen or by pressing the side button again.

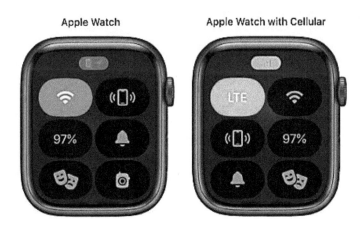

Apple Watch

Apple Watch with Cellular

Icon	Description	For more information
((ᣮ))	Turn cellular on or off—Apple Watch models with cellular only.	See Set up and use cellular service on Apple Watch.
🛜	Disconnect from Wi-Fi.	See Disconnect from Wi-Fi.
🧑‍🏫	Turn on Schooltime—managed Apple Watch models only.	See Set up Schooltime.
((☐))	Ping your iPhone.	See Ping your iPhone (Apple Watch Series 8 and earlier) and Ping and find your iPhone (Apple Watch Series 9 only).
100%	Check your battery percentage.	See Charge Apple Watch.
🔕	Silence Apple Watch.	See Turn on silent mode.
🔒	Lock your watch with a passcode.	See Lock or unlock Apple Watch.
🎭	Turn on theater mode.	See Use theater mode on Apple Watch.
((◎))	Make yourself available for Walkie-Talkie.	See Use Walkie-Talkie on Apple Watch.
🌙	Choose a Focus/Do Not Disturb.	See Create a Focus schedule.
👤	Turn off Personal Focus.	See Create a Focus schedule.
💼	Turn off Work Focus.	See Create a Focus schedule.
🛌	Turn off Sleep Focus.	See Track your sleep with Apple Watch.

Turn on the flashlight.	See Use the flashlight on Apple Watch.
Turn on Airplane Mode.	See Turn on Airplane Mode.
Turn on Water Lock.	See Go for a swim with Apple Watch.
Choose audio output.	See Connect Apple Watch to Bluetooth headphones or speakers.
Check headphone volume.	See Connect Apple Watch to Bluetooth headphones or speakers.
Change text size.	See Adjust brightness and text on Apple Watch.
Turn Accessibility Shortcuts on or off.	See Set the Accessibility Shortcut.
Turn Announce Notifications on or off.	See Listen and respond to incoming notifications with AirPods and Beats headphones on Apple Watch.

The Status Of The Control Center May Be Checked.

At the very top of Control Center, you'll notice a number of icons that show you the current status of various settings. For example, you can check whether your Apple Watch is connected to cellular, if an app is utilizing your location, and if Airplane Mode or Do Not Disturb are activated.

To access the Control Center and see the icons representing the various statuses, press the side button. To get additional details, use the icons.

Reorganize Command Post

The following instructions will show you how to rearrange the buttons in the Control Center:

- Pressing the side button will bring up the Control Center.
- After you reach the very bottom of the Control Center, click Edit.
- You can move buttons around by touching and holding them.
- When you're through, click the Finish button.

Remove Control Center Buttons

In order to remove the Control Center buttons, follow these steps:

- Pressing the side button will bring up the Control Center.
- After you reach the very bottom of the Control Center, click Edit.
- Pick out the button you want to remove and then hit the Delete button in the corner of it.
- When you're through, click the Finish button.

Open Control Center, go to Edit and then press the Add button on the right side of the button you want to restore. Hit the Finish button once you're done.

Turn On Airplane Mode

By setting your Apple Watch and iPhone to Airplane Mode, you may be able to travel with them switched on with certain airlines. Airplane Mode disables Wi-Fi and cellular (on Apple Watch models that support cellular) while leaving Bluetooth on by default. But when you activate Airplane Mode, you may choose which settings are enabled and disabled.

- The Apple Watch's Airplane Mode may be activated by pressing the side button to access

Control Center, followed by tapping the Airplane Mode button.

Turn Airplane Mode on or off.

Assistant Siri: Just say, "Activate Airplane Mode."

Put Your Apple Watch And Iphone Into Airplane Mode At The Same Time: On your iPhone, open the Apple Watch app and go to General > Airplane Mode. Once you've done that, press on My Watch. Turn on Mirror iPhone lastly. Once one device enters Airplane Mode, all of the other devices within the usual Bluetooth range of each other will do the same—roughly 33 feet or 10 meters.

Modify How To Turn On Or Off The Airplane Mode: By navigating to the Settings app, selecting Airplane Mode, and finally selecting the option, you may program your Apple Watch to automatically turn Wi-Fi and Bluetooth on or off whenever you engage Airplane Mode.

Toggle the state of your Apple Watch's Wi-Fi or Bluetooth by opening the Settings app and touching on the corresponding button. If you're using Airplane Mode on your watch, this will come in handy.

When you toggle Airplane Mode on, you'll see the icon for it at the very top of your screen.

Note: You still need to disable Airplane Mode on both your iPhone and Apple Watch individually, even when you have Mirror iPhone enabled. The status of the Control Center may be checked.

Make Use Of Apple Watch's Built-In Flashlight

Light up a dark door lock, let people know you're going for a nighttime run, or illuminate surrounding items without damaging your night vision with the help of the flashlight.

- Pressing the side button opens the Control Center; to activate the flashlight, press the Flashlight button. By swiping left, you may choose between three modes: steady red light, flashing white light, and stable white light.

- Simply left-or right-turning the Digital Crown will adjust the brightness.
- To disable the flashlight, press the side button, use the Digital Crown, or swipe downward from the top of the watch display.

Put Your Apple Watch Into Theater Mode.

The Apple Watch display remains black in theater mode because it is disabled from coming on when you lift your wrist. You may still get haptic alerts even when it goes on quiet mode and disables your Walkie-Talkie status.

After opening Control Center with the side button press, choose Theater Mode by tapping the button.

Turn theater mode on or off.

You can tell if theater mode is active by looking for the status indicator in the upper-right corner of the screen.

Tap the screen, push the side button or the Digital Crown, or flip the Digital Crown to wake up the Apple Watch in theater mode.

Get Off The Wi-Fi

If your Apple Watch is cellular-enabled, you may quickly switch to using an available cellular connection by disabling Wi-Fi in the Control Center.

Tap the Wi-Fi button after opening the Control Center by pressing the side button.

Tap to disconnect from Wi-Fi.

For a short while, your Apple Watch will no longer be able to connect to Wi-Fi. When you're within range of your Apple Watch's cellular network, the connection will activate. Your Apple Watch will automatically rejoin the Wi-Fi network the next time you go back to the same location unless you've accidentally erased the connection from your iPhone.

Hint: Press and hold the Wi-Fi button in the Control Center to swiftly access your Apple Watch's Wi-Fi settings.

Put The Phone On Quiet Mode.

Launch Control Center by pressing the side button; then, choose Silent Mode by tapping the button.

Be aware that even when set to silence, your Apple Watch's alarms and timers will continue to ring while it is charging.

Put your Apple Watch into silent mode by opening the app on your iPhone. Then, choose Sounds & Haptics from My Watch.

At the first sound of any beep from your Apple Watch, placing your palm on the screen and holding for three seconds will quickly stop it. A tap will indicate that you have activated mute. Navigating to the Settings app, selecting Sounds & Haptics, and ultimately activating Cover to Mute will allow you to use your Apple Watch.

Ping Your iPhone (Apple Watch Series 8 And Earlier)

If your iPhone is in the area, your Apple Watch can assist you in locating it.

Next, press the Ping iPhone button after opening the Control Center with the side button.

So you can find it, your iPhone makes a noise.

Tip: When it's dark? Holding down the Ping iPhone button will also cause your iPhone to flash.

Use Find My on iCloud.com to see whether your iPhone and Apple Watch are within range of one other.

Ping And Find Your iPhone (Apple Watch Series 9 Only)

With Precision Finding, your Apple Watch Series 9 can locate your nearby iPhone 15 and provide you with instructions for it.

- The Ping iPhone button is accessible on the Apple Watch Series 9 via the side button, which opens the Control Center.

  When your Apple Watch Series 9 is close enough, your iPhone will make a noise and show you the approximate direction and distance to your watch, like 77 feet.

- Locate it by tapping the Ping iPhone button in the bottom-right corner, or by using your iPhone's built-in sound capabilities.
- Make course corrections following the on-screen heading.

  The watch face will glow green and you'll hear two beeps from your iPhone as soon as you get near it.

Tip: When it's dark? Holding down the Ping iPhone button will also cause your iPhone to flash.

Use Find My on iCloud.com to see whether your iPhone and Apple Watch are within range of one other.

Please be aware that not all areas provide Precision Finding.

Reach Out To Your Apple Watch

If your Apple Watch is in the area, you may use your iPhone running iOS 17 to locate it.

+ Launch the iPhone's Settings app.
+ After swiping down in the Control Center, find Ping My Watch and press the Add button.

- To access Control Center on your iPhone, scroll down from the top-right corner to see it. From there, hit the Ping Apple Watch button whenever you want to ping your Apple Watch.

Note: If you own several Apple Watches, the audio will be played on the watch that is marked in the "All Watches" section of the Apple Watch app on your iPhone.

CHAPTER FOUR

HOW TO ORGANIZE APPS ON APPLE WATCH SERIES 9

Sort Your Applications In A Grid.

- ◆ Pressing the Digital Crown on your Apple Watch will take you to the Home Screen.

  To go to grid view from list view, slide down from the top of the screen. Another option is to go to the Apple Watch's Settings app, go to App View, and finally, touch on Grid View.

- ◆ To move an app to a different spot, touch and hold it.
- ◆ Finish by pressing the Digital Crown.

Touch and hold an app, then drag to a new location.

For the iPhone version, you may access the Apple Watch app by opening it, tapping My Watch, then tapping App View, and finally tapping Arrangement. You can move app icons around by touching and holding their icons.

Note: that applications are always shown in alphabetical order in the list view.

Touch and hold an app, then drag to a new location.

Remove An App From Apple Watch

To uninstall an app from your Apple Watch, press and hold the Home screen until the X appears. You can't remove it from your linked iPhone unless you also remove it from that device.

Swipe left on the app in list view, then press the Trash button to erase it from your Apple Watch.

Once you uninstall an app from your iPhone, it will also be removed from your Apple Watch. Any app, even those built into Apple products, can be restored by downloading it from the App Store on an Apple Watch or iPhone.

Please be aware that not all applications are erasable from the Apple Watch.

Play Around With The App's Parameters

- On your iPhone, launch the Apple Watch app.
- Scroll down to view the apps you installed after tapping My Watch.
- To access the settings of an app, touch on it.

Your Apple Watch will also be impacted by some of the limitations that you establish on your iPhone under Settings > Screen Time > Content & Privacy Restrictions. If you turn off the Camera app on your iPhone, for instance, the Apple Watch will no longer display the Camera Remote icon.

Verify The Capacity Of Apps' Storage

You can see how much space is being used on your Apple Watch's storage, including the total amount, the amount that is left, and the percentage that each app uses.

- Go to your Apple Watch's Settings.
- Under General, choose Storage.

Alternative methods include launching the Apple Watch app on an iPhone, selecting My Watch, and then navigating to General > Storage.

HOW TO INSTALL MORE APPS ON APPLE WATCH SERIES 9

Your Apple Watch comes with a plethora of apps that may track your health, exercise, communications, and even the passing of time. Additionally, the App Store can be accessed via an Apple Watch or iPhone, allowing users to install third-party apps or download new ones. All of your apps are housed on the Home Screen.

Be aware that the Settings app on your Apple Watch allows you to activate Automatic Downloads. Once you do so, any app you've installed on your watch will immediately download the iOS version. Enabling Automatic Updates ensures that your Apple Watch apps are constantly up-to-date.

Add Applications To Your Apple Watch Via The App Store.

- Launch Apple Watch's App Store.

- Discover highlighted applications and collections by turning the Digital Crown.
- To see more applications, tap on a collection.
- Select "Get" to get a free app. Just press the price to purchase an app.

  You may download the software again without paying if the Download button appears instead of a fee. Having the iOS version of an app installed on your iPhone is often necessary for some applications.

To start searching, go to the top left of the screen and click the Search symbol. Next, either manually enter the program's name (on compatible models only; not available in all languages) or input it using Scribble or voice commands. Popular app categories may also be accessed by tapping on them.

Use it on any of these compatible devices by swiping up from the bottom and tapping Scribble.

Note: that cellular data costs may apply while using Apple Watch with cellular. Unfortunately, not all languages are supported by Scribble.

Put Your Existing Iphone Applications Into Action.

Your iPhone will automatically install and display any applications that have a watchOS app by default. Alternatively, you may use these procedures to install certain apps:

- On your iPhone, launch the Apple Watch app.
- Turn off Automatic App Install by tapping My Watch, then General.
- Select Available Apps after tapping My Watch.
- Select the applications you want to install, and then tap Install.

HOW TO SET TIMERS ON APPLE WATCH SERIES 9

For accurate timekeeping, download the Timers app for Apple Watch. Timer intervals of up to 24 hours may be programmed into various devices.

"Set a timer for 20 minutes," you may tell Siri.

Easy Timer Setup

- Pull up the Tmers app on your trusty Apple Watch.
- Select a timer you've used before (such as 1, 3, or 5 minutes) or choose a duration from the options below Recents to start a timer fast. After that, use the Add button to make your watch.

When one timer goes off, you may set another one to go off at the same time by tapping the Repeat Timer button.

Stop Or Start A Timer

- Get the Timers app for your Apple Watch going while a timer is in the background.
- You may stop the video, continue it, or terminate it by using the appropriate buttons.

Make Your Timer

- Pull up the Timers app on your trusty Apple Watch.
- Select the plus sign.
- Turn the Digital Crown to change the time, or press the hour, minute, or second buttons.
- Press the Start button.

Tap hours, minutes, or seconds, then turn the Digital Crown.

Make Several Timers

1. Pull up the Timers app on your trusty Apple Watch.
2. Get a timer going.

Hint: When you use Siri to establish a timer, you may attach a name like "Pizza" to it. Promptly set a 12-minute pizza timer by raising your Apple Watch and speaking into it.

3. You may start a new timer by tapping the Add button, which will take you back to the Timers interface.

Pressing the Back button will bring up the Timers panel, where you can see your running timers. To put a timer to sleep, just press the Pause button; to bring it back to life, press the Play button.

When a timer is shown on the Timers screen, you may remove it by swiping left and then tapping the X.

HOW TO SET ALARM ON APPLE WATCH

Set An Alarm On Your Apple Watch With Siri

Similar to the iPhone, Apple Watch may be asked to set an alarm by Apple's digital assistant.

Note: Although the specifics of your Apple Watch's menu may vary from model to model, the fundamentals of alarm setup are the same across the board.

1. Verify that your Apple Watch has Siri turned on. Find Siri in the Settings menu. You have three options for activating Siri: Press the Digital Crown, Raise to Speak, and Hey Siri.

2. "Hey Siri, set an alarm for 6:15 PM," or "Set repeating alarm for 5 pm daily," will instruct Siri to begin setting an alarm. "Set an alarm for 45 minutes from now" or "Set a weekend alarm for noon" are examples of relative time.

How To Set An Alarm On Apple Watch

Additionally, your Apple Watch has touch capabilities that allow you to set an alarm.

1. The alarm is the orange clock symbol on the face of your watch. Press it.
2. Go to the Add Alarm setting.

Note: If you have many alarms set, you may have to scroll down to see this one.

3. To set the alarm to a certain hour, turn the Digital Crown to that setting. To alter the time, hit the minutes box and spin the Crown again. You may pick the time of day by selecting AM or PM.
4. Your new alarm will appear in your Apple Watch's alarm list when you choose Set.

5. To activate or deactivate your alarm, just touch the green toggle.

6. Once you've decided on an alarm time, you may customize it by selecting options like Repeat, Label, and Snooze.

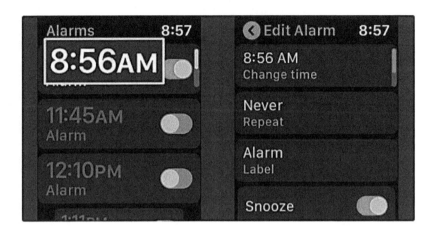

Setting Your Alarm Clock To Never Go Off

Another simple feature of the Apple Watch is the ability to delete or cancel alarms.

1. Your Apple Watch's Alarm app should launch.
2. To remove an alarm, just pick it up.
3. Tap Delete when you reach the bottom of the page. If you erase it by accident, you will have to recreate the alarm since there is no confirmation stage.

Configure Your Alarm To Receive Push Notifications

If you set an alarm on your iPhone, it will also show up on your Apple Watch.

1. After opening the Apple Watch app on your iPhone, go to the bottom left corner and tap on My Watch.
2. Toggle the switch for iPhone Push Alerts to the green state once you scroll down and choose Clock.

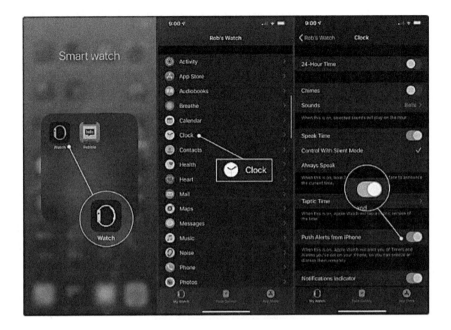

You may now snooze or disregard an alert without moving your hand off your wrist anytime an alarm on your iPhone goes off—all thanks to your Apple Watch. Your iPhone will not get a notification when your Apple Watch notifies you.

Use Nightstand Mode To Deactivate Your Apple Watch's Alarm

While your Apple Watch is in Nightstand Mode, you may snooze or ignore the alarm that you've set.

1. Lie your Apple Watch on its side with the crown and buttons facing upwards. The

current time, the battery life, and the next alarm time you've set are all shown.

2. Pressing the Side button will turn off the alarm entirely while pressing the Digital Crown will snooze it for nine minutes.

CHAPTER FIVE

HOW TO RESPOND TO NOTIFICATION ON APPLE WATCH SERIES 9

Apple Watch notifies you of upcoming events and allows you to react to them. Notifications may come from a variety of sources, including meeting invites, texts, noise alarms, and activity reminders. If you don't have time to read a notice when it comes in, your Apple Watch will store it for later.

React To An Alert As Soon As It Shows Up

1. Raise your wrist to see any alerts that come your way, whether they're audible or not.

   When the screen is active or not, the notice will appear differently.

   In An Active Display: A little banner is shown at the very top of the screen.

   During Inactivity: A notice takes up the whole screen.

2. View the notice by tapping on it.

3. Swipe down on a notice to dismiss it. You may also press Dismiss when you scroll down to the bottom of the notice.

View Messages To Which You Have Not Yet Replied

In the event that a notice remains unresponsive after first receipt, notice Center will keep track of it. A red dot will show up at the top of your watch face to signify that you have unread notifications. You can see it if you do this:

1. Swipe down from the top of the watch face to access the Notification Center. Swipe down from other displays by touching and holding the top of the screen.

Note: The Apple Watch Home Screen does not allow you to access the Notification Center. Alternatively, you may access the Notification Center by pressing the Digital Crown, which will take you to the watch face or launch an app.

2. To navigate through the list of alerts, either swipe up or down or use the Digital Crown.
3. To view or reply to the notice, tap on it.

Hint: Whether you're listening on your Bluetooth headphones or the speaker built into your Apple Watch, Siri can read out loud any alerts that appear in the Notification Center. "Read my notifications" is all it takes.

Swiping to the left and tapping X will remove a notice from the notice Center even if you haven't read it. Navigate to the top of the screen and choose Clear All to erase all alerts.

A group may be opened by tapping on it, and then you can press on a notification to enable group notifications.

Hint: go into your Apple Watch's Settings, then touch Notifications. From there, you can disable the

Notifications Indicator, which will prevent the red dot from showing on the watch face.

Swipe down to view unread notifications.

Turn Off All Alerts On Your Apple Watch.

Launch Control Center by pressing the side button; then, choose Silent Mode by tapping the button.

A notification still hits you with a tap. To stop noise and tapping, do the following:

- Open Control Center by pressing the side button; then, choose the Do Not Disturb or Focus option.
- By tapping the Do Not Disturb button, you may choose an option to keep the device silent for an hour, till today evening, or until tomorrow morning.

To swiftly silence your Apple Watch whenever it beeps, just put your hand on the screen and hold it there for three seconds. When you turn on mute, you'll feel a tap. You can activate Cover to Mute in the Apple Watch's Settings app. Just go to Sounds & Haptics and toggle it on.

HOW TO CHANGE NOTIFICATION SETTINGS ON APPLE WATCH SERIES 9

When you first set up your Apple Watch, its notification settings will be identical to those on your iPhone. However, the notification appearance in certain applications may be customized.

Note: A family member's Apple Watch that you are managing will not have its settings mirrored.

Pick The Method Your App Uses To Notify Users

1. On your iPhone, launch the Apple Watch app.
2. Press on Notifications after tapping My Watch.
3. After selecting the app (e.g., Messages), hit Custom, and finally, pick an option. Alternatives might involve:
   - As soon as you enable notifications, the app will show you any new messages in the Notification Center.

- Notifications are routed straight to the Notification Center instead of being seen or audible on your Apple Watch when you choose this option.
- Turn off push notifications for this app.

4. Set the preferred method for categorizing app alerts. Possible choices are:

- *Turned Off:* Notifications are not categorized.
- *In An Instant:* With the use of app data, your Apple Watch can categorize your activities. Your news alerts, for instance, are organized according to the channels you're following, such as CNN, the Washington Post, and People.
- All of the app's alerts are categorized by app.

Advice: You can customize the alerts you get from certain applications. For instance, under Calendar, you have the option to enable alerts for certain calendars or activities, such as when someone modifies a shared calendar or sends you an invitation. In Mail, you have the option to choose which email addresses may get alerts.

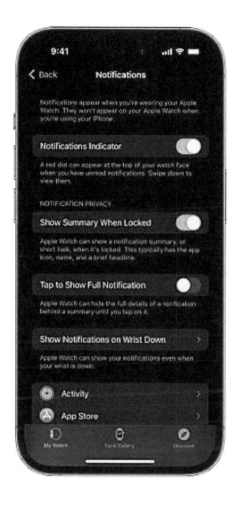

Manage Your Apple Watch's Notifications Without Ever Leaving The Watch.

By pressing the More button or swiping left on a notice, you may modify various notification choices directly on your Apple Watch. Alternatives might involve:

- If you want to silence your Apple Watch for the next hour or all day, you may do that by directing messages to the Notification Center instead of sending them immediately to your wrist. By swiping left on a notice, tapping the More icon, and then tapping Unmute, you may restore the ability to see and hear these notifications.
- Enhance the Summary: Your iPhone's Notification Summary will display any future app alerts.
- Get the app to inform you right away again by opening the Settings app on your iPhone, tapping Notifications, tapping the app, and finally tapping Immediate Delivery.
- Even if you're using a Focus that delays most alerts, time-sensitive notifications will always be sent promptly until you turn off time-sensitive. Nevertheless, you may disable the app's ability to send any kind of notification, including time-sensitive ones, by tapping this option.
- On, the app will no longer give you push notifications. Navigate to the following steps in the Apple Watch app on your iPhone: open the app, hit My Watch, then choose Notifications. From there, select the app

whose settings you need to modify, and finally, press Allow Notifications.

Allow Alerts To Be Shown On The Lock Screen

The Apple Watch's lock screen is customizable, so you can decide how alerts show there.

1. Go to your Apple Watch's Settings.
2. Select Notifications.
3. Please choose one of the following:
   - When you turn this feature on, your Apple Watch will display a summary of notifications whenever it is locked. The name and emblem of the alerting app are

included in the summary, along with a short headline.

- When you lift your wrist to read a notice, you'll first get a summary. A few seconds later, you'll see the complete contents. To see them all, tap the notification. Take incoming messages as an example; you'll initially see the sender's name before the message itself shows. To prevent the whole notice from showing until you touch it, enable this option.

- If you want alerts to show up on your Apple Watch while your wrist is down, you may change the default setting to do so. To have alerts shown even when you're not wearing your Apple Watch, enable this feature.

CHAPTER SIX

HOW TO MANAGE YOUR APPLE ID SETTINGS ON APPLE WATCH SERIES 9

Take Control Of Your Apple ID On The Go With The Apple Watch

All of the data linked to your Apple ID is editable. A trustworthy phone number, updated contact details, a new password, and more are all within your reach.

Revise Private Data

1. Go to your Apple Watch's Settings.
2. Choose an option from the following after tapping [your name] on Personal Information:
   - ***Change Your Name:*** To sort your name from first to last, touch on it.
   - ***Find Out A New Birthday:*** After selecting Birthday, input a new date.
   - ***Sign Up For Announcements, Suggestions, Or Apple News:*** To access the communication preferences, tap on that option. Notifications, apps, music, and TV suggestions, as well as the Apple News Newsletter, may be activated.

GET CONTROL OF YOUR APPLE ID'S SECURITY SETTINGS

1. Go to your Apple Watch's Settings.
2. Select Sign-In & Security after tapping [your name].

   You can see all the contact information (primary or verified) and status (email and phone) linked to your Apple ID here.

3. Perform one of these tasks:
   - **Decreasing A Confirmed Email Address:** To remove an email address, tap on it and then press Remove.
   - **Kindly Provide Contact Information (Phone Numbers And Email Addresses):** To add an email or phone number, choose the option and then click Next. After entering the information, hit Done.
   - **Log In With A New Apple ID:** Select Change Password and then adhere to the prompts shown on the screen.
   - **You May Edit Or Add A Reliable Phone Number:** To remove a trusted phone number, go to Two-Factor Authentication, touch on your current number, confirm when asked, and then hit

Remove Phone Number. If you only have one trusted number, you'll need to add a new one first. Select Add a Trusted Phone Number to add another trusted number.

- **Find Out How To Get A Verification Number So You Can Log In On Icloud.Com Or Another Device:** To get a verification code, go to Two-Factor Authentication and then tap on Go.
- **Modify The "Sign In With Apple" Preferences For A Website Or App:** Next, choose an app by tapping the "Sign in with Apple" button. To remove the app's association with your Apple ID, tap Stop Using Apple ID. (The next time you attempt to log in via the app, you may be prompted to establish a new account.)
- **Not Show My Email:** Select an address and then press Forward To.

Enabling this feature enables applications to communicate with you without saving your actual email address. If you go with this choice, Apple will generate a random email address only for you; later on, the app will send emails written to this address instead of the one you provided.

- **Learn About The Current State Of The Recovery Key:** Finding out if your Apple ID has a Recovery Key setup is important.

If you're using two-factor authentication and have an Apple device, you may strengthen the security of your account by creating a recovery key on your iOS device. Your recovery key will allow you to access your Apple ID if you need to reset your password.

See All Of Your Subscriptions And Control Them

- Go to your Apple Watch's Settings.
- Press on [your name].
- Scroll down to see your current and expired memberships after tapping memberships.
- To see the price, duration, and subscription choices for a certain subscription, just tap on it.
- Hit the Cancel Subscription button to terminate your membership.

Keep in mind that you can't cancel all subscriptions using your iPhone.

When a subscription expires, you may resubscribe by touching the icon and selecting a new subscription period, such as monthly or annually.

KEEP TABS ON ALL OF YOUR GADGETS

- Go to your Apple Watch's Settings.
- Press on [your name].
- Tap a gadget to see its details after scrolling down.
- Click Remove from Account if the gadget doesn't seem familiar.

HOW TO CONNECT APPLE WATCH SERIES 9 TO A WIFI NETWORK

Join An Existing Wi-Fi Network With Your Apple Watch.

You can keep using your Apple Watch's functions even when you're not near your iPhone by connecting it to a Wi-Fi network.

Select A Wireless Network

1. To access the Control Center, press the side button.
2. To connect to a wireless network, press and hold the Wi-Fi button until a list of networks appears.

Only 802.11b/g/n 2.4GHz Wi-Fi networks are compatible with the Apple Watch.

3. Select an option if a password is required to access the network:
   - For models that enable it, you may use the Apple Watch's keyboard to input the password; however, not all languages are supported.
   - The characters for the password may be scribbled on the screen using your finger. To change the case of a character, just click and hold the Digital Crown.
   - Select a password by tapping the Password button.
   - Enter the password using the on-screen keyboard on your iPhone.
4. Press the Join button.

TURN APPLE WATCH INTO A PRIVATE NETWORK NODE.

Every time your Apple Watch connects to a Wi-Fi network, it assigns itself a distinct private address, or media access control (MAC) address, to aid with privacy protection. You have the option to discontinue utilizing a private address for a network if it is unable to do so for any reason, such as providing parental controls or authenticating your Apple Watch as an approved joiner.

1. To access the Control Center, press the side button.
2. Press and hold the Wi-Fi button until the network you just joined appears.
3. Stop using Private Addresses.

Note: Private Address enabled for all networks that allow it for improved privacy. When you connect your Apple Watch to a private network, it becomes more difficult for other networks to follow it.

Set Aside A Network

1. To access the Control Center, press the side button.
2. Press and hold the Wi-Fi button until the network you just joined appears.
3. Click on the "Forget This Network" button.

You will need to input the password again if the network asks for one when you reconnect to it later.

CHAPTER SEVEN

HOW TO CONNECT APPLE WATCH TO BLUETOOTH HEADPHONES OR SPEAKERS

Utilize Bluetooth headphones or speakers to play music from your Apple Watch even when your iPhone isn't in the room.

Advice: Just hit play to begin using your AirPods on your Apple Watch once you've connected them up with your iPhone.

LINK WIRELESS EARBUDS OR SPEAKERS

The speaker on the Apple Watch plays most audio, including Siri, phone calls, voicemail, and voice notes, but you'll need Bluetooth headphones or speakers to hear all of this. To activate the exploration mode, follow the on-box instructions for your headphones or speakers. Once the Bluetooth device is prepared, proceed as follows:

1. Launch the Apple Watch's Settings app and go to Bluetooth.
2. When the gadget displays, tap on it.

Additionally, the Audiobooks, Music, Now Playing, and Podcasts apps all include AirPlay buttons on their play screens that may be used to access the Bluetooth settings.

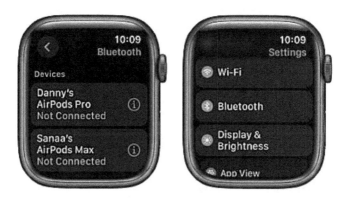

Select A Sound Output Device.

+ To access the Control Center, press the side button.
+ Select your desired audio output device by tapping the Audio Output icon.

LISTEN TO YOUR HEADPHONES AND CHANGE THE LEVEL.

+ To access the Control Center, press the side button.
+ Press the Headphone Volume button while your headphones are turned on.

A meter displays the current level of the headphones.

- Adjust the volume by tapping the slider or the settings located under Headphone Volume; alternatively, you may use the Digital Crown.

Reduce Loud Sounds

You may restrict the volume of your headphones to a certain decibel level using the Apple Watch.

- Go to your Apple Watch's Settings.
- To lower the volume, open the Sounds & Haptics menu, then choose Headphone Safety.
- Select a level and then activate Reduce Loud Sounds.

LISTEN TO ALERTS ON YOUR HEADPHONES WITH A HIGH VOLUME

To prevent damage to your hearing, Apple Watch will alert you when you've been listening to too loud music on your headphones for an extended period and will then automatically reduce the volume to a more comfortable level.

Here are the procedures you need to take to get information regarding headphone notifications:

- Go to your Apple Watch's Settings.

- Select Last 6 Months from the drop-down menu under Headphone Notifications in Sounds & Haptics > Headphone Safety.

Accessing the Health app on an iPhone is another option; from there, go to Hearing, Headphone Notifications, and finally, tap on a notification.

HOW TO USE AIRPODS AND OTHER BLUETOOTH ACCESSORIES WITH APPLE WATCH

Find out how to connect a variety of wireless accessories to your Apple Watch, including headphones and heart rate monitors.

Connect Your Bluetooth Device

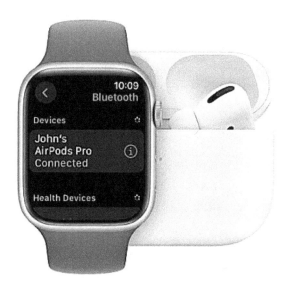

- Follow the on-product instructions to put your Bluetooth device into pairing mode.
- Select Bluetooth from the Apple Watch's Settings menu. When you're close to another Bluetooth device, your Apple Watch will look for it.
- Pick out a Bluetooth device.
- Punch in a passcode or PIN if prompted.

Detach Your Bluetooth Peripheral.

- Select Bluetooth from the Apple Watch's Settings menu.
- Locate your Apple Watch attachment and tap the info icon.
- Click the "Forget Device" button.

Use Your Airpods' Connection

Set up your AirPods using your iPhone, and they'll sync with your Apple Watch and iPhone at the same time, allowing you to enjoy music from either device without lifting a finger.

Seek Assistance

If your Bluetooth item isn't connecting or won't reconnect:

- ♦ Your watch is in Airplane Mode if the word "Airplane" appears on the face. Simply disable

Airplane Mode by going to your Apple Watch's Settings and tapping on it.

- Verify that the item is both switched on and completely charged.
- If you are unable to connect the accessory despite seeing it in Apple Watch's Settings > Bluetooth, follow the instructions above to unpair it.
- Give pairing the accessories another go.

HOW TO SET AND USE CELLULAR SERVICE ON APPLE WATCH SERIES 9

When you have an Apple Watch with cellular and connect it to the same carrier as your iPhone, you can do a lot more without an iPhone or Wi-Fi, including make calls, respond to messages, utilize Walkie-Talkie, stream music and podcasts, get alerts, and more.

Note: Not all places or carriers provide cellular coverage.

UPGRADE YOUR CELLULAR PLAN WITH THE APPLE WATCH.

Just follow the on-screen prompts when you first set up your Apple Watch to enable cellular data. Here are the procedures to activate the service at a later time:

1. On your iPhone, launch the Apple Watch app.
2. Press Cellular on your watch's menu.

To activate cellular on your Apple Watch and find out more about your carrier's plans, just follow the on-screen directions.

Move Your Current Mobile Plan To Your New Apple Watch.

To move your current cellular plan from one Apple Watch with cellular to another, you need to follow these steps:

- Launch the Apple Watch app on your iPhone when you're wearing your wristwatch.
- Select Cellular from the menu on your wristwatch. Then, locate your cellular plan and hit the Info button.
- After you confirm your option, tap the "Remove [name of carrier] Plan" button.

  Removing this Apple Watch from your cellular plan could require you to contact your provider.

- Take off your old watch. Step 2: Put on your new cellular Apple Watch. Next, touch My Watch. Finally, hit Cellular.

Turn on your watch's cellular capabilities by following the on-screen prompts.

Switch The Cellular On Or Off.

The Apple Watch that supports cellular data will use the most optimal network connection at its disposal, which may be your iPhone if it's close by, a Wi-Fi network that you've already established on your iPhone or cellular data. For reasons like conserving battery life, you may disable cellular data. Here are the simple steps:

- To access the Control Center, press the side button.
- To toggle Cellular on or off, press and hold the Cellular button.

When your Apple Watch is connected to cellular data and your iPhone isn't in range, the Cellular button will glow green.

Note: Keeping cellular data enabled for long periods drains the battery faster. For additional details, see the Apple Watch General Battery Information page. Some applications won't let you update them unless you're connected to your iPhone.

DETERMINE THE QUALITY OF THE CELL SIGNAL.

If you're on a cellular network, try this:

- To see how strong your cellular signal is, use the Explorer watch face. Four dots make a solid link. Poor one dot.
- Turn on the Command Center. The state of the cellular connection is shown by the green bars at the top.
- The Cellular complication should be shown on the watch face.

Evaluate The Use Of Mobile Data

- Go to your Apple Watch's Settings.
- Find your current data use by tapping Cellular and then scrolling down the screen.

HOW TO SET UP CELLULAR ON APPLE WATCH

Even when you're not near your iPhone, you can use your Apple Watch's cellular connection to do things like make calls, respond to messages, and get alerts.

Before Beginning

- Always use the most recent software updates for your Apple Watch and iPhone.
- Make sure your carrier settings are up-to-date.

- Get a cellular plan with a carrier that is compatible with this device. To activate cellular connectivity on your Apple Watch, you need to be in the range of your carrier's network and your iPhone must be using the same carrier.
- Get in touch with your business or cellphone provider to find out whether this feature is compatible with your plan. We are unable to assist with pre-paid or older accounts at this time. Get in touch with your service provider to verify account eligibility.

Tip: You may give a family member an Apple Watch that works with a different carrier than your own iPhone.

CONFIGURE APPLE WATCH'S CELLULAR SERVICE

During the initial setup of your Apple Watch or another family member's watch, you have the option to enable cellular data. Find the cellular setup option during setup and follow the onscreen instructions.

Additionally, the Apple Watch app allows you to configure cellular at a later time:

- Launch the Apple Watch on your iOS device.

- Select Cellular from the My Watch menu.
- Navigate to the Cellular Setup menu.
- Pay attention to the directions provided by your carrier. For assistance, you should probably get in touch with your carrier.

The phone number associated with your Apple Watch may be different from the one associated with your iPhone. Your carrier will only use the number shown on your Apple Watch for billing or tracking reasons. The number is the same for both your iPhone and Apple Watch.

Confirm The Apple Watch's Cellular Connectivity With A Loved One.

If a loved one doesn't possess an iPhone, you can still help them stay connected with a cellular Apple Watch. You will be prompted to add the managed Apple Watch to your plan during setup if your cellular provider allows it. Find the cellular setup option and follow the on-screen instructions. Using a different carrier may be an option if your current one does not offer cellular on a controlled Apple Watch.

You may add cellular functionality to a family member's Apple Watch at a later time:

- On your iPhone, launch the Apple Watch app.
- Pick out a family member's Apple Watch by tapping All Watches, then choose Done.
- Choose Cellular, and then choose Set Up Cellular.
- Pay attention to the directions provided by your carrier. For assistance, you should probably get in touch with your carrier.

Once your family member has activated cellular on their Apple Watch, you can see their allocated phone number by going to Settings > Phone on the watch.

Limited availability applies to the ability to set up a managed Apple Watch for a family member in certain countries or areas.

Note: Local restrictions in China mainland demand you to authenticate your identification while setting up cellular on a family member's Apple Watch. For more help, get in touch with your carrier.

Join A Cellular Service

If your Apple Watch is cellular-enabled, it will automatically choose the most energy-efficient wireless network: If your iPhone is close, connected to a Wi-Fi network, or using cellular, it can connect to it. The watch takes advantage of LTE networks whenever it establishes a cellular connection. As an alternative to LTE, your watch will attempt to connect using UMTS if it is supported by your carrier.

You can see the strength of the signal via the Control Center or the Cellular complication that most watches allow you to add when your watch connects to a cellular network. Swipe up from the bottom of the screen after touching and holding it to launch Control Center.

You can tell you have a connection when the Cellular button goes green. The signal strength is shown by the green bars.

Even if your watch is linked to your iPhone over Bluetooth or Wi-Fi, the Cellular button flashes white when your cellular plan is active.

CHANGING CARRIERS

Unless another member of your family doesn't own an iPhone, you'll need to ensure that your Apple Watch and iPhone are on the same carrier. Your Apple Watch will need to deactivate the old service plan and activate the new one if you switch iPhone carriers.* Give it a try:

- Launch the Apple Watch on your iOS device.
- Select Cellular from the My Watch menu.
- When you change the carrier on your iPhone, your Apple Watch should also change to match. Simply press the "Add a New Plan"

button and follow the on-screen instructions to create a new plan. You can delete your old plan from the Apple Watch app if it's still there. Talk to your service provider if you're stuck.

Switch To A New Apple Watch And Keep Your Existing Mobile Plan.

You can move your cellular data from your old Apple Watch to your new one when you're ready to start using it. Give it a try:

- Deactivate the cellular service from your previous Apple Watch. Either use the Apple Watch app or factory reset your previous Apple Watch to do this.
- Connect your brand-new Apple Watch to your iOS device. Add a cellular plan by tapping "Set up Cellular" during setup.
- From the Apple Watch app, you may transfer your current plan to your new Apple Watch with certain carriers.
- Get in touch with your service provider if you are unable to locate a method to switch your phone plan.

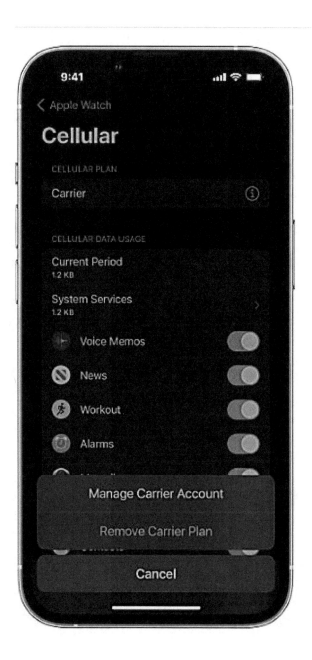

DISCONTINUE YOUR MOBILE SERVICE

At any moment, you may cancel your phone plan:

- Launch the Apple Watch on your iOS device.
- Select Cellular from the My Watch menu.
- At the top of the screen, you should see your cellular plan. To see more details, tap on that icon.
- To cancel your [carrier] plan, press the corresponding button. Verify by tapping once more.
- To terminate your mobile service, you may have to get in touch with your provider.*

The option to deactivate the plan is available when you wipe and unpair your Apple Watch. Select Erase All when prompted to delete the whole plan.

There can be carrier surcharges. To find out more, call your provider.

Using Your Apple Watch For International Roaming

Apple Watch Series 5, Apple Watch SE, and Apple Watch Ultra cellular versions are eligible for foreign roaming with watchOS 9.1 and later.

You may add your Apple Watch to your iPhone's cellular roaming plan by contacting your iPhone carrier. This will enable your watch to get worldwide roaming capabilities. Your Apple Watch won't be able to use international roaming unless your carrier supports VoLTE and roaming. The extent to which your Apple Watch is covered when you go abroad is dependent on your carrier, and not all of them enable international roaming.

Launch the Apple Watch's Settings app to enable international roaming. To enable Data Roaming, tap Cellular.

CHAPTER EIGHT

HOW TO USE ASSISITIVETOUCH ON APPLE WATCH SERIES 9

If you have trouble making physical contact with the Apple Watch's screen or buttons, AssistiveTouch may assist. You can use your hand movements to accept calls, move an on-screen pointer, and access a menu on your Apple Watch, thanks to its built-in sensors.

These and other tasks may be accomplished with the help of AssistiveTouch gestures:

- Hit the screen
- Use the on-screen rotating digital crown
- Make quick screen swaps
- Retain the on/off button
- Gain access to the Control Center, Notification Center, and the App Switcher.
- Display software programs
- Make payment with Apple Pay
- Verify each side button press with two clicks
- Bring up Siri
- Enter a shortcut for Siri

Important: Enabling AssistiveTouch on Apple Watch Series 9 disables the universal double tap gesture.

SET UP ASSISTIVE TOUCH

1. Go to your Apple Watch's Settings.
2. Accessibility > AssistiveTouch is where you'll find the toggle to activate the feature.
3. To activate Hand Gestures, tap on that feature.

   Hint: you can see a list of all the available hand gestures underneath the Hand Gestures toggle; tapping "Learn more" will bring up an explanation of each one. To learn and master a motion, just touch on it, and an animated tutorial will pop up.

Alternatively, you may activate AssistiveTouch by opening the Apple Watch app on your iPhone, tapping My Watch, and then navigating to Accessibility > AssistiveTouch.

USE ASSISITIVETOUCH WITH APPLE WATCH

When you activate AssistiveTouch and hand gestures on your Apple Watch, you may use these motions to navigate:

- Forward pinch
- Two pinches: rear
- Knock: Press
- Double-click to bring up the menu of options

To demonstrate how to utilize AssistiveTouch with the Activity app, these are the steps to take while the Meridian watch face is displayed:

1. For AssistiveTouch to work, double-press the screen.
   Around the Music's complexity, a spotlight emerges.
2. The Activity complication may be accessed by pinching three times, and then tapping it requires clenching.
3. To access the Action Menu, double-press the Activity app's icon when it launches.
4. Select the System action with a single pinch, the Scroll Up action with a second squeeze, and finally, clench to pick it.
5. Press the Clench button to get to the next screen.
6. To access the Action Menu, just double-press.
   You can advance through the activities by pinching, and you can rewind them by double-pressing.

7. After choosing the Press Crown action, you may go back to the watch face by clenching it once.

Use The Motion Pointer

The Motion Pointer adds to the pinching and gripping capabilities of your Apple Watch the ability to manipulate it by tilting it up and down and side to side. For instance, here's how to utilize the Motion Pointer in the Stopwatch app:

- To enable AssistiveTouch, double-press when the watch face is visible.
- The Action Menu will appear when you double-click once more.
  This action will be chosen: Press Crown.
- To access the Home screen, press and hold the Crown icon.
- To access the Action Menu, double-press the screen twice. Pinch to go to the Interaction action, and then double-press to touch it.

  Choose the Motion Pointer option.

- Select "Motion Pointer" from the menu.
  The screen displays a cursor.
- Position the pointer at the screen's bottom edge by tilting the watch; then, scroll down.

- The Stopwatch app may be opened by briefly holding the cursor over it.
- Press the start button by holding the mouse pointer over it.
- Press the crown with a squeeze, double-clench to reveal the Action Menu, and then clench to return to the watch face.

Use Quick Actions

When an alert appears on your Apple Watch, you may reply quickly by using quick actions. For instance, a notification informs you that you may answer incoming calls by double-pressing the screen. while your Apple Watch senses motion that seems like it may be a workout, you can start a workout with a single tap, and while the Camera app's viewfinder and shutter button are visible, you can snap a picture with a single tap as well. Here are the methods to enable or disable fast actions.

- Go to your Apple Watch's Settings.
- Find Quick Actions under Accessibility and choose one.

  Depending on your preference, you may decide whether fast actions are always accessible, available just when AssistiveTouch is turned on, or disabled. There are two more options: Full appearance (which highlights the action button and displays a banner) and Minimal appearance (which highlights the action button without the banner).

Tip: By tapping "Try it out," you may practice the rapid actions gesture.

MODIFY THE ASSISTIVETOUCH PREFERENCES

You can modify the sensitivity of the Motion Pointer, customize the behaviors associated with pinching and clenching, and more.

To use the AssistiveTouch feature, open the Apple Watch's Settings app and go to Accessibility. After that, you may perform one of the following:

- You may personalize gestures by going to Hand Gestures, tapping on a gesture, and then selecting an activity or a Siri shortcut.
- Select Motion Pointer from the menu, and then tweak the sensitivity, activation time, movement tolerance, and hot edges settings to your liking.
- Style of scanning: Pick between Automatic scanning, in which each action is highlighted automatically, or Manual scanning, in which you transition between them using gestures.

- Visually, you may make the highlight stand out more by activating High Contrast. Select a new highlight color by tapping Color.
- Menu Personalization: Choose your preferred actions, move and resize the Action Menu, and alter the auto scroll speed.
- Enable AssistiveTouch to confirm payments with the password or if double-clicking the side button is necessary.
- Other options include opening the Apple Watch app on an iPhone, tapping My Watch, and then navigating to Accessibility > AssistiveTouch.

HOW TO USE SIRI ON APPLE WATCH SERIES 9

Useful Siri Commands

Your Apple Watch may become an extension of your phone with the help of Siri. Take Siri as an example: she can translate your speech into many languages, instantly identify songs with Shazam, and show you the top search results with a little extract from each page when you ask a general query. With a simple touch, you may access the website on your Apple Watch. If you generally have to accomplish things by hand, try utilizing Siri instead.

Siri isn't localized to every country or language. For further information on the availability of watchOS features, be sure to see the Apple Support page.

Siri: What would you say?

- "What is the Chinese translation of 'How are you?'?"
- "Get going on a 30-minute run outside."
- "Please inform Kathleen that I am nearly done."
- Awaken your sleeping app.
- "Access Preferences"
- "Mine, which tune is this?"
- I asked, "What causes rainbows?"
- I'm sorry, but I don't have an update.
- "May I inquire about something specific?"

HOW TO USE SIRI

Choose one of these options to ask Siri a question:

- Speak into your Apple Watch simply by raising your wrist.

  To disable Raise to Speak, go to your Apple Watch's Settings, then touch Siri. From there, you can choose to disable the capability.

- Just say "Hey Siri" (or "Siri") and then your request.

  To disable "Ask Siri," go to your Apple Watch's Settings app, then touch Siri. From there, choose Listen for "Siri" or "Hey Siri," and finally, pick Off.

  Several languages and places do not support the use of "Siri" exclusively.

- To make a voice request, press and hold the Digital Crown until the listening indication appears.

  Navigate to the Apple Watch's Settings app, choose Siri, and finally, disable the Press Digital Crown function.

Advice: You may let your wrist droop after you've activated Siri. If there is a reaction, you will feel a tap.

While holding down the Digital Crown, you may ask Siri a question or carry on the discussion.

Just like on iOS, iPadOS, and macOS, Siri can talk back to you. An Apple Watch-connected Bluetooth headset or speakers may also amplify Siri's voice answers.

Note: You'll need an internet connection for Siri to work on your Apple Watch. Cellular fees could be applicable.

HOW TO DETERMINE SIRI'S RESPONSE STYLE

Your Apple Watch can receive voice answers from Siri. Navigate to the Apple Watch's Settings app, then choose Siri. From there, touch on Siri Responses. From the list of options, select:

- Even when your Apple Watch is set to mute, Siri will continue to voice replies.
- When you put your Apple Watch into quiet mode, Siri will not respond.

- If you're using Bluetooth headphones with your Apple Watch, Siri will only respond by voice.

Navigate to the Settings app on your Apple Watch, then choose Siri. From there, choose Language or Siri Voice to customize the language and voice used by Siri. You may choose a new speech type by tapping Siri speech.

Note: Not all languages have the ability to modify Siri's voice.

Show The Transcripts And Captions Of Your Siri Commands.

You may see Siri's transcriptions and subtitles of your commands and replies on your Apple Watch. To toggle Always Show Siri Captions and Always Show Speech on or off, go to the Apple Watch's Settings app, then select Siri. Then, hit Siri Responses. Scroll down to the bottom of the page.

Type To Siri And Siri Pause Time

You may ask Siri to wait longer or write a request if you're having trouble speaking.

- Go to your Apple Watch's Settings.

- To enable Type to Siri, go to Accessibility > Siri.
- Select Longer or Longest from the Siri Pause Time menu if you want Siri to hold on for a longer period while you talk.

Clear Siri's Cache

Apple stores your requests made to Siri or via dictation for six months to enhance Siri's ability to respond to you. Your Apple ID and email address are not linked to your requests; instead, a random identifier is. These exchanges are permanently removed from the server.

- Go to your Apple Watch's Settings.
- To delete your Siri history, open Siri, then hit Siri History.

CHAPTER NINE

HOW TO SET UP AND VIEW YOUR MEDICAL ID

A medical ID lists your allergies, current medical problems, emergency contacts, and any other information that might be used in the event of an emergency. In the event of an emergency, this information may be seen on your Apple Watch or iPhone and your emergency contacts can be contacted by Emergency SOS through satellite.

MAKE YOUR UNIQUE MEDICAL ID.

In the Health app, create a Medical ID.

1. Take out your iPhone and launch the Health app.
2. Select Medical ID after tapping your profile image in the upper right.
3. To begin, choose Edit or Get Started, and then input your details.
4. To add contacts, go to the Emergency Contacts section and hit the plus sign.

   Unless you decide to disable this feature, your iPhone will notify your emergency contacts via text message after an emergency call finishes.

While in SOS mode, your iPhone will notify those who have asked to be notified of your whereabouts if your position changes, and it will also communicate your current location if it is accessible.

5. Press Finish.

Hint: Press and hold the Health app icon on the Home Screen to access Medical ID.

Give First Responders And Emergency Agencies Permission To Use Your Medical ID.

In the event of an emergency, your medical information will be immediately shared (inside the United States and Canada only), and it will also be shown on the Lock Screen of your Apple Watch and iPhone.

- Take out your iPhone and launch the Health app.
- Select Medical ID after tapping your profile image in the upper right.
- Scroll down to the bottom of the Edit screen, and then toggle the Show When Locked and Emergency Call options on.

Important: For a first responder to access your Medical ID, you must first unlock your iPhone by swiping up or touching the Home button (whichever is your model), then tap Emergency on the passcode screen, and last select Medical ID.

HOW TO VIEW YOUR MEDICAL ID ON APPLE WATCH SERIES 9

Your medical history, including any allergies or diseases you may have, as well as any other pertinent information, may be found on a medical ID. Your Apple Watch will have access to the same medical records that you enter into your iPhone's Health app. When you dial 911, send a text message, or utilize Emergency SOS (available in the US and Canada only), your Apple Watch may transmit your medical records to the emergency services you've designated.

So that medical personnel responding to you in an emergency can see your Medical ID, your Apple Watch can show it.

Read the section on "Set up and view your Medical ID" in the iPhone User Guide to find out how to configure your Medical ID on the go.

Just follow these instructions to access your Medical ID on your Apple Watch:

1. The sliders will not show until you press and hold the side button.
2. Turn the Medical ID dial to the right.
3. Hit the Finish button once you're done.

HOW TO CUSTOMIZE SAFETY FEATURES ON APPLE WATCH SERIES 9

There are many types of emergencies when your Apple Watch might be useful.

- ***Show Important Medical Information On Apple Watch:*** Create a Medical ID and have it show up on your Apple Watch's lock screen to display crucial medical information. Your age, blood type, medical issues, and allergies may be seen by those attending you in the event of an emergency. Refer to Apple Watch allows you to set up and see your medical ID.

- ***Get In Touch With The Paramedics:*** You may access emergency services, Siri, or Messages by pressing and holding the side button on your Apple Watch. In the event of an emergency, you may notify loved ones by adding emergency contacts on your phone. Review the information about how to get in touch with emergency assistance.

- **If You See A Hard Fall, Call 911 Immediately:** Enabling Fall Detection on your Apple Watch enables it to assist in contacting emergency personnel. Visit the Apple Watch page for further information on how to manage fall detection.

- **In The Event Of A Serious Vehicle Accident, Notify The Appropriate Authorities Immediately:** You can help notify emergency services if your Apple Watch Series 8, Apple Watch SE (2nd Generation), or Apple Watch Series 9 detects a serious automobile collision.

HOW TO MAKE APPLE WATCH CRASH DETECTION WORK FOR YOU

After a serious vehicle accident, your Apple Watch Series 8, Series 9, or Apple Watch SE (2nd Generation) can assist you get in touch with emergency personnel and alert your emergency contacts.

After 20 seconds of notifying you of a serious vehicle accident, your Apple Watch will begin dialing 911 until you tell it to stop. Your latitudinal and longitudinal coordinates, together with an estimated search radius, will be sent to emergency personnel in an audio message that plays if you are unresponsive. The recording notifies them that you have been in a major automobile collision.

If you want to contact emergency services, you'll need an iPhone or Apple Watch that is either connected to a cellular network or has Wi-Fi calling enabled and accessible.

Crash Detection alerts to emergency services may be conveyed using the Emergency SOS via satellite system if cellular and Wi-Fi coverage is unavailable and your Apple Watch is near your iPhone 14 or later. This feature is accessible in areas where Emergency SOS via satellite is available. If you want to know how to use Apple's Emergency SOS feature on your iPhone, check out this Help page.

Important note: In the event of a serious vehicle accident, Crash Detection will not supersede any prior emergency calls made via other channels.

Enable Or Disable Crash Detection

By default, Crash Detection is enabled. Here are the methods to disable Apple's warnings and automated emergency calls after a serious automobile crash:

- Go to your Apple Watch's Settings.
- To disable Call After Severe Crash, go to SOS > Crash Detection.

HOW TO CHANGE THE WATCH FACE ON YOUR APPLE WATCH SERIES 9

Make your Apple Watch appear and perform exactly as you want it to by customizing the face. Pick a layout, personalize it with your choice of colors and features, and then add it to your library. To see the correct timekeeping tools or to change things up, you may switch faces at any time.

The Apple Watch app's Face Gallery is the simplest method to peruse all of the face options, personalize one, and add it to your collection. You can change the face of your watch without ever taking your iPhone out of your pocket. View Apple Watch faces and features for additional information.

Select An Alternative Timepiece Face

Select the desired watch face by touching and holding it, swiping on it, and then tapping it.

Swipe left or right to see other watch faces.

Simple

Add features to your watch face.

EXTEND THE WATCH FACE WITH ADDITIONAL FEATURES

Some watch faces allow you to attach additional features, called complications, that allow you to quickly access things like the weather, stock prices, or information from other applications you've loaded.

- When the watch face is shown, press and hold the screen to bring up the Edit menu.
- Complete the gesture by swiping left.
  On the final screen, you'll see any faces that present issues.
- To access other complications, such as Activity or Heart Rate, you may tap on one to pick it and then use the Digital Crown to change it.
- You may save your modifications by pressing the Digital Crown after you're done. To swap faces, just touch on the screen.

Complicating matters further are some of the applications available in the App Store.

Optional Complications For The Apple Watch

Pressing a watch face complication will launch the majority of applications. Some intricacies display data from a single app, allowing you to quickly get the information you need. Air quality, circumstances, temperature, and other factors are all part of weather.

Several intricacies are shown by the following applications.

App	Available complications
Activity	Rings
	Timeline
Astronomy	Earth
	Moon
	Solar
	Solar System
Calendar	Today's Date
	Your Schedule
Compass	Compass
	Elevation
	Level
Compass Waypoints	Last Viewed Waypoint
	Saved Waypoints
	Parked Car Waypoint

Home	Home
	Grid Forecast
Maps	Maps
	Get Directions
Mindfulness	Mindfulness
	State of Mind
Reminders	Due Today
	Reminders
Sleep	Data
	Data and Schedule
	Sleep
Stocks	Added Stocks
	Last Viewed Stocks
Time	Analog Seconds
	Analog Time
	Digital Seconds
	Digital Time

Maps	Maps
	Get Directions
Mindfulness	Mindfulness
	State of Mind
Reminders	Due Today
	Reminders
Sleep	Data
	Data and Schedule
	Sleep
Stocks	Added Stocks
	Last Viewed Stocks

Time	Analog Seconds
	Analog Time
	Digital Seconds
	Digital Time
Timer	Added Timers
	Timer
Weather	Air Quality
	Conditions
	Humidity
	Rain
	Temperature
	UV Index
	Wind
World Clock	Sunrise/Sunset
	Added Locations

ENHANCE YOUR COLLECTION WITH A NEW WATCH FACE

You may make your own set of unique faces, including variants on the same design.

- Press and hold the screen while the present watch face is shown.
- To add a new one, swipe left until you reach the end, and then press the plus sign.
- Press Add after using the Digital Crown to choose a watch face.

Hint: You may narrow your search for watch faces by tapping on a collection, such as New Watch Faces or Artists.

The watch face may be customized after adding it.

Tap new, scroll to browse watch faces, then tap a face to add it.

Peruse Your Assortment

At a glance, you may see all of your watch faces.

- On your iPhone, launch the Apple Watch app.
- After tapping My Watch, go down to My Faces and swipe through your collection.

Drag the Reorder icon next to a watch face to move it up or down in your collection. You may do this by tapping Edit in My Faces.

On the Apple Watch, you may also change the sequence of your collection. While the present watch face is visible, press and hold the screen once again, and then drag the chosen watch face to the left or right.

Remove A Model From Your Portfolio

- Press and hold the screen while the present watch face is shown.
- To remove a face, just swipe to it, lift it, and hit the Remove button.

Another option is to use the Apple Watch app on your iPhone. Once inside, touch My Watch. Then, under the My Faces section, hit Edit. Select all of the watch faces you want to remove, then hit the Delete button.

Adding the watch face is something you can do at a later time.

Swipe up to delete a watch face, then tap Remove.

Before You Set The Watch,

- Go to your Apple Watch's Settings.
- Pull down the clock screen.
- To advance the watch by up to 59 minutes, press +0 min and then use the Digital Crown.

This option just modifies the time that appears on the watch face; it does not affect alarms, notification times, or any other times (like World Clock).

CHAPTER TEN

HOW TO USE CAMERA REMOTE AND TIMER ON APPLE WATCH

With the latest version of watchOS, you can set up your iPhone for a picture or video shoot, and then use your Apple Watch to capture the shot or video remotely. The three-second pre-shoot delay is the default, so you have time to drop your wrist and raise your gaze before the photo is taken.

Within the typical Bluetooth range of an iPhone— roughly 33 feet or 10 meters—your Apple Watch may serve as a camera remote.

Siri: Just say, "Take a picture."

Choose options.

Take a photo.

Snap A Picture

1. Launch the Camera Remote Apple Watch app.
2. With the help of your Apple Watch, you can position your iPhone such that it frames the photo.

   Use the Digital Crown to adjust the zoom. To change the exposure, touch the important part of the photo in the preview.

3. You may snap a picture by pressing the shutter button.

You may examine the snapshot on your Apple Watch, even if it was recorded on your iPhone.

Capture Footage

Using the Camera Remote app on your iPhone, you can capture video with your watchOS 10 device.

1. Launch the Camera Remote Apple Watch app.
2. With the help of your Apple Watch, you can position your iPhone such that it frames the photo.

   Use the Digital Crown to adjust the zoom.

3. To begin recording, press and hold the Shutter button.
4. To end the recording, let go of the shutter button.

Evaluate Your Images

To go over your photos on your Apple Watch, just follow these steps.

- Go through an image: Select the slider located in the lower left corner.
- Explore other images by swiping left or right.
- Use the digital crown to zoom in.
- To pan, just drag the zoomed image.
- Use the whole screen: Click and hold the snapshot twice.

- Make the Close button and shot count visible or hidden: Press the screen.

Select Close when you are finished.

1. Try adjusting the parameters on a different camera.
2. Launch the Camera Remote Apple Watch app.

Select an option from the list that appears when you tap the More Options button:

- Timers (three-second on/off)
- Headshot or backshot
- Beam (automatic, on, or off)
- On/Off Live Photo Mode

HOW TO MAKE PHONE CALLS ON APPLE WATCH SERIES 9

Use Apple Watch's Siri to make phone calls: Use language like:

- He said, "Call Max."
- "Telephone 555 555 2949."
- "Make a FaceTime call to Pete."

Make A Call

- Launch the handset's phone app on the wristwatch.

- Drag the Digital Crown to navigate through the contacts, then tap on them.
- After selecting the person you want to contact, just touch the phone button.
- To initiate an audio call using FaceTime, either touch the audio icon or enter the phone number.
- To change the volume while on the phone, simply turn the Digital Crown.

Advice: Go to Recents, then touch on a contact, to dial the number of someone you've just talked with. In the iPhone's Phone app, go to Favorites, then touch a contact to call a person you've marked as a favorite.

Send Out A Group Facetime Message.

You may now use your Apple Watch to join group FaceTime audio chats with the latest version of watchOS.

- Launch the handset's phone app on the wristwatch.
- Launch an audio call using FaceTime.
- Please choose one of the following options to add more participants to the reservation:

- Select a contact by tapping the Add People option after tapping the More Options button.
- Select a contact by tapping 2 People Active, then the Add button at the screen's bottom, if someone has joined the call.

You have the option to have a second person on the call even if you didn't initiate it. Select a contact by tapping 2 People Active, then either tapping Add People or the Add button.

On The Apple Watch, Type In A Phone Number.

- Launch the handset's phone app on the wristwatch.

- Launch an audio call using FaceTime.
- Go to the More Options menu, and then choose the Add People option.

While on the phone, you may input more numbers using the keypad. To access the keypad, just press the More Options button.

Communicate Wirelessly

Your Apple Watch can replace your cellular network with Wi-Fi for making and receiving calls, even when your associated iPhone isn't nearby or turned off if your cellular provider supports this feature. If your iPhone has already connected to a Wi-Fi network, all your Apple Watch needs is to be in the range of that network.

- You may enable Wi-Fi calling on this iPhone and add Wi-Fi calling for other devices under the Settings > Phone menu on your iPhone.
- Launch the handset's phone app on the wristwatch.
- After selecting a contact, just press the Call button.
- Figure out the number or FaceTime location you want to contact.

Note: Although you may make calls in an emergency using Wi-Fi, it is recommended to utilize your iPhone via a cellular connection for the most precise location data. Just briefly turning off your Apple Watch's Wi-Fi will do the trick.

View My Call History On My Apple Watch

Using the Phone app on your Apple Watch, you can see incoming and outgoing calls simultaneously with your iPhone. When you're not using your phone—say, with a headset or earphones—you may easily cancel the conversation using your Apple Watch.

HOW TO PLAY MUSIC ON APPLE WATCH

If you own an Apple Watch, you can listen to music by downloading the Music app. Listen to music on your Apple Watch, manage your iPhone's music library, and even stream Apple Music if you have a subscription.

Siri: could you just say:

+ "Listen to Victoria Monét's 'Party Girls.'"
+ "I want to hear more music from this album."
+ "Cue up my exercise music.'"
+ "City of Apple Music Play"

- "Insound some smooth jazz."
- "Chorus of songs for a formal dinner"
- "To unwind, I'd like to listen to a playlist."
- "Keep up the good work."

Start Playing Some Music

Tap for more options.

Once your Apple Watch is linked to Bluetooth headphones or speakers, launch the Music app and choose from the following options:

- *Use Your Apple Watch To Listen To Music:* Use the Digital Crown to navigate the Listen Now screen; then, choose an album, playlist, or category by tapping on it.

  To transfer music to your Apple Watch, use the Apple Watch app on your iPhone.

- *From The Listen Now Screen, Go To The Back Button:* Then, hit Library. From there, pick a category like Playlists, Albums, Downloaded, or a newly added item. Then, choose music to play.
- *If You Have An Apple Songs Membership, You May Request Songs From The Service:* Just raise your wrist to request a certain artist, album, song, genre, or even a lyric excerpt.
- *Browse The Music Collection On Apple Music:* Just type in the name of an album, musician, or song and hit the Search button. Press on an outcome to hear it.

Get Some Tunes Playing

Customized music playlists are available to Apple Music subscribers.

1. Launch Apple Watch's Music app.
2. You may see the songs you've recently uploaded to your Apple Watch and a personalized feed of albums and playlists according to your tastes if you scroll down.
3. After selecting a genre, album, or playlist, you may play them by clicking the Play button.

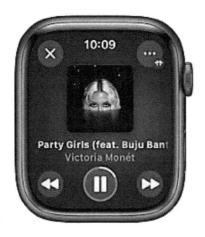

Start The Line

You may see a list of forthcoming tracks in the queue while playing music.

1. Launch Apple Watch's Music app.
2. Select Playing Next from the More Options menu after starting a song or playlist.
3. To play a song from the queue, just touch on it.

When you turn on Auto Play, related songs will automatically be added to the queue. Pressing the Auto Play button will disable Auto Play.

Note: Disabling Auto Play on an Apple ID-using gadget (such as an Apple Watch) will have a one-time effect. Unless you individually off Auto Play on each device, it will keep running on all of them.

You may add songs, playlists, or albums to your queue by swiping left on them, tapping the More icon, and then selecting Play Next or Play Last. If you want to play music at the very end of the queue, you have to pick it last.

Manage The Playing Process

You may change the volume by using the Digital Crown. Here are the ways to play music on your iPhone and Apple Watch:

▷	Play the current song.
‖	Pause playback.
▷▷	Skip to the next song.
◁◁	Skip to the beginning of the song; double-tap to skip to the previous song.

Hint: Press the Now Playing screen to conceal the controls.

Mute Or Play The Same Song Again

- Through the playback screen, you may shuffle or replay songs: To access the playback controls, use the More Options option, then

Playing Next. From there, you can choose between Shuffle and Repeat.

To play a song again, press the Repeat button twice.

If you're an Apple Music member, Autoplay will automatically add songs that are similar to the one you were listening to before to the end of your queue. You may disable Autoplay by tapping the button.

- Sort the songs in your collection by mood: From the Now Playing screen, go to the Library by tapping the Back button. From there, choose Artists, Albums, or Songs. Finally, press on Shuffle All.

Listen To Tunes With An Alternative Gadget

When you link your Apple Watch with headphones or any other Bluetooth-enabled device, including speakers or other headphones, you can listen to music wirelessly. Additionally, you may manage your music library using Apple TV and HomePod speakers—devices that are compatible with AirPlay.

Choose one option from the following on the Now Playing screen after tapping the More Options icon in the upper right:

- To pair with a Bluetooth accessory, open the AirPlay menu, press Choose a Device, and then choose the appropriate device.
- Hit AirPlay, then hit Control Other Speakers & TVs. Select a device, and finally, select some music to play.

A Speedy Way To Go Back To The "Now Playing" Screen

The Now Playing button is located in the upper right corner of the Music app and may be tapped from any screen. If the display of the watch is visible, raise the Digital Crown, and then either push the Music button located at the top of the screen or the Smart Stack to access the currently playing song.

HOW TO ADD MUSIC TO APPLE WATCH

You can listen to music on your Apple Watch even when you're not near your iPhone—just add songs to it.

Using the Apple Watch app on your iPhone, you can add individual albums and playlists to your Apple Watch. Additionally, the songs app allows Apple Music subscribers to add songs straight to their Apple Watch.

If you have an Apple song subscription, you may add any song you choose to your Apple Watch. It will automatically add the music you've been listening to lately. (Apple Music's recommendations will be added if you haven't listened to anything yet.)

IMPORT TUNES FROM YOUR IPHONE

- On your iPhone, launch the Apple Watch app.
- Move to Music by tapping My Watch.
- Click on "Add Music" at the bottom of the Playlists & Albums screen.
- Tap the Add button to add albums and playlists to the Playlists & Albums queue after navigating to the locations where you want to connect your Apple Watch.

The Apple Watch will sync with your iPhone to play music.

Hint: If you own an iPhone, you may use the Music app to make playlists tailored to the music you want to play on your Apple Watch. This can be useful for creating workout-specific playlists, for instance. For information on how to make a playlist in Apple Music, check out this post from Apple Support.

SYNC UP YOUR TUNES WITH YOUR APPLE WATCH

With an Apple Music subscription, you may sync your music library with your wristwatch.

1. Launch Apple Watch's Music app.
2. To add music to Listen Now, go to the screen where you may do that.

   Alternatively, you may search for songs to add by tapping the Back button, then Search, from the Listen Now interface.

3. To add a playlist or album to your library, touch on it, then hit the More Options option.

   The addition of the item is confirmed with a message.

Attention: With an active internet connection, you may listen to music stored on your Apple Watch wirelessly. You have to download music before you can listen to it offline.

4. Once you've tapped the More Options option, you may download the music to your Apple Watch.

Important: When your Apple Watch isn't plugged into an electrical outlet, downloading music drains more battery than usual.

The Apple Watch Can Now Have A Music Playlist.

With the Apple Watch's Workout app, you can sync your music collection to play in the background whenever you begin a workout.

1. On your iPhone, launch the Apple Watch app.
2. Move to Workout by tapping My Watch.
3. Press the Workout Playlist icon and choose a playlist.
4. In the Apple Watch app on your iPhone, go to My Watch > Music and add the playlist.

Note: It is not possible to listen to a workout playlist simultaneously with any other audio or music.

HOW TO USE WALKIE-TALKIE ON YOUR APPLE WATCH

Use the Walkie-Talkie app to tap to connect, whether you're out shopping or trying to locate someone in a crowd. You may control the time you wish to speak and add pals.

Walkie-Talkie requires an Apple Watch Series 1 or later running watchOS 5.3 or later on both your end and your friend's end. Additionally, you must both have an iPhone running iOS 12.4 and can initiate and receive FaceTime audio conversations.

INSTRUCTIONS FOR ADDING CONTACTS TO THE WALKIE-TALKIE

1. Launch the Apple Watch Walkie-Talkie app.
2. You may send an invitation by scrolling through the contact list and tapping on a name.
3. Just hang tight till your pal says yes. You won't be able to see their gray contact card under "Friends You Invited" until they accept your invitation. Your friend's contact card will

become yellow when they accept, allowing you to start a conversation right away.

Launch the Walkie-Talkie app, swipe left on a buddy, and then press the Delete symbol to remove them. Another option is to launch the Apple Watch app on your iPhone. Then, go to Walkie-Talkie > Edit. From there, hit the minus button and then choose Remove.

HOW TO ACCEPT A WALKIE-TALKIE INVITATION

When prompted, tap the "Always Allow" option in the invitation notice. See whether the alert pops up in the Notification Centre if you don't see it the first time. Also, the Walkie-Talkie app will show you the invitations.

What To Say To Start A Walkie-Talkie Chat

1. Launch the Apple Watch Walkie-Talkie app.
2. Tap a friend
3. Press and hold the "talk" button until you can speak. Hold tight until the Walkie-Talkie connects if the word "connecting" appears on the screen. Your buddy may immediately start talking to you when Walkie-Talkie has connected.

If your buddy is sporting an Apple Watch and has the Walkie-Talkie feature on, they will be notified whenever you want to initiate a conversation.

The Walkie-Talkie Way To Communicate

1. Press and hold the speak button until you utter a word.
2. After you're done, release the button. Your companion will immediately pick up on your words.

Use the Digital Crown to adjust the loudness.

DISABLE OR ACTIVATE THE WALKIE-TALKIE.

1. Launch the app for the walkie-talkie.
2. Enable or disable the walkie-talkie. A notice will show asking whether you would want to speak if someone attempts to call you while you are not available.

Additionally, the Walkie-Talkie button in the Control Centre may be used to toggle the Walkie-Talkie on and off.

The chimes and your friend's voice will continue to be audible even after you switch to Silent Mode in the Control Centre. You will no longer be able to use the Walkie-Talkie when you switch to Theatre Mode. By simulating your iPhone's settings, Do Not Disturb lets you choose when and which Walkie-Talkie notifications display.

CHAPTER ELEVEN

TIPS AND TRICKS

1. Return To The Clock

Holding up your wrist doesn't necessarily have to show you the time if you have an app you'd prefer to display instead. You may change the on-screen app by going to Settings > General > Return to Clock, regardless of whether your screen is always on or not.

Please go to the section labeled "On Screen Raise Show Last" by scrolling down. There are four options: Always, While in Sessions, Within an hour of Last Use, and two minutes of Last Use.

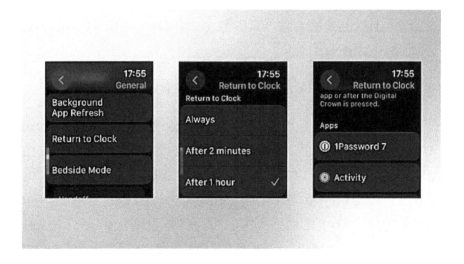

2. Resize The Text Shown On The Screen

Apple has made the accessibility option available in case you want a bigger font on your rather little gadget. To change the brightness, go to the Settings menu and choose Display & Brightness.

If reading the time in big numbers is all that matters to you, a specialized Big Text watch face is an option.

3. Use Your Palm To Silence Notifications

If you want to silence the Watch's notifications, you may do so by turning off the sound feature.

If it goes off in an unexpected spot, you may quickly silence it by covering the screen for three seconds or longer. Navigate to My Watch > Gestures > Cover to Mute in the Apple Watch app on your iPhone to activate the option.

4. Disable Watch Applications

To hide third-party applications from your Apple Watch, open the Apple Watch app on your iPhone and go to the My Watch area. Find "Installed on Apple Watch" at the bottom of the page. To remove an app, tap on it and then turn off the toggle. Unless you also remove them from your iPhone, these applications will be loaded on your Watch even after you remove their interfaces.

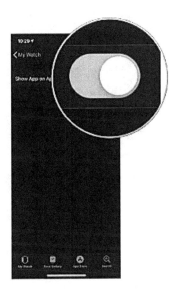

5. Use The Watch To Locate Your iPhone

Is your iPhone missing? The good news is that you can use your Apple Watch to find it. Press the side button on your Apple Watch. Here you may make it sound so you can find it easier by tapping the blue Ping button on the iPhone.

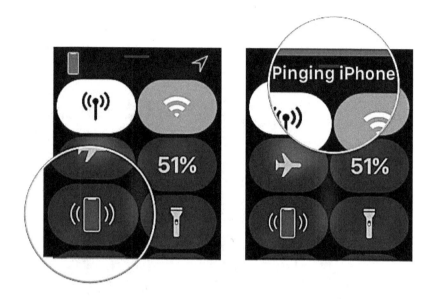

6. Get To Zoom And Voiceover With Ease.

Making your iPhone's critical capabilities, like Zoom or VoiceOver, accessible on your Apple Watch is a breeze. To have Zoom or VoiceOver launch automatically, enable the Accessibility shortcut (three clicks). The Apple Watch app on an iPhone is where you'll find this option; from there, choose My Watch > Accessibility > Accessibility Shortcut. Here you may choose which one you want to activate automatically whenever you triple-click.

By just speaking to your Watch, you may also tell Siri to activate or deactivate VoiceOver.

7. Grab A Screen Capture

Feel like snapping a picture of your Digital Touch creation, whether it is an activity accomplishment or something more whimsical? To capture a screenshot, press and hold the side button and the Digital Crown at the same time.

8. Restart The Apple Watch By Force.

Holding down the side button until you see the emergency orders will disable your Watch if it starts acting up. Drag the Power Off toggle to the left after tapping the power button on the right. Holding the side button and Digital Crown for 10 seconds or until you see the Apple logo can forcibly reset your Watch if it has completely frozen.

9. Store Your Watch Faces

With the use of Force Touch on the Watch screen, you may personalize the preset faces provided by Apple and even store your faces for later use. If that's what you're after, just press and hold the Watch screen again, swipe left, and then hit the "New" button. The updated version of your watch face is now fully customizable.

Swipe up to remove a personalized watch face.

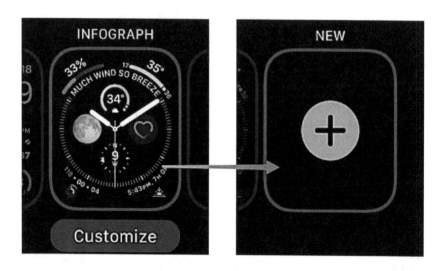

10. Add Five Minutes To The Speed Of Your Watch.

If you want to be punctual for every meeting and appointment, the Apple Watch may help you achieve that goal. Like showing up promptly for scheduled appointments? You may manually adjust the time display to show five minutes faster (or more) without affecting your alarms, alerts, or global clocks. The display on your Watch is all that matters. Turn the Digital Crown to travel up to 59 minutes ahead of the current time, or go to Settings > Clock > +0 min.

11. Disable The Snooze Feature On Your Alarms.

Turning off the snooze feature will wake you up immediately if you're not confident in your ability to get up at the appointed hour. You may adjust the alarm time by going into the device's Alarm app and tapping on the desired time. If you want to force yourself to get going, you may toggle the snooze option.

www.ingramcontent.com/pod-product-compliance
Lightning Source LLC
LaVergne TN
LVHW051326050326
832903LV00031B/3393